JANET MELROSE &
SHERYL NORMANDEAU

The Prairie Gardener's Go-To for

Seeds

T0160333

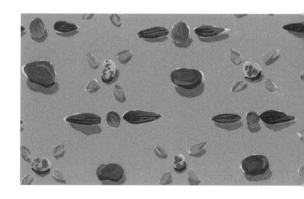

TOUCHWOOD

Copyright © 2021 by Janet Melrose and Sheryl Normandeau

All rights reserved. No part of this publication may be reproduced, stored in a retrieval system, or transmitted in any form or by any means, electronic, mechanical, photocopying, recording, or otherwise, without the prior written permission of the publisher. For more information, contact the publisher at:

TouchWood Editions
touchwoodeditions.com

The information in this book is true and complete to the best of the authors' knowledge. All recommendations are made without guarantee on the part of the authors or the publisher.

Copy edited by Paula Marchese

Design and illustration by Tree Abraham

Photos by Janet Melrose and Sheryl Normandeau with the following exceptions: p. 35 (by Pascale Gueret / Shutterstock.com) and p. 66 (by Sirachai Chinprayoon / Shutterstock.com).

CATALOGUING DATA AVAILABLE FROM LIBRARY AND ARCHIVES CANADA

ISBN 9781771513449 (print)

ISBN 9781771513456 (electronic)

TouchWood Editions acknowledges that the land on which we live and work is within the traditional territories of the Lkwungen (Esquimalt and Songhees), Malahat, Pacheedaht, Scia'new, T'Sou-ke and W̱SÁNEĆ (Pauquachin, Tsartlip, Tsawout, Tseycum) peoples.

We acknowledge the financial support of the Government of Canada through the Canada Book Fund, and the province of British Columbia through the Book Publishing Tax Credit.

This book was produced using FSC®-certified, acid-free papers, processed chlorine free, and printed with soya-based inks.

Printed in China

25 24 23 22 21   1 2 3 4 5

Dedicated to all prairie gardeners

Introduction 7

Introduction

Let's get sowing!

For anyone who has ever put a seed into the ground and watched it germinate and grow, the whole process is a cause for celebration. Who hasn't felt that huge amount of satisfaction and joy, seeing those little shoots pop up out of the soil? If you're new to gardening and haven't experienced these moments yet, you'll understand exactly what we're talking about when it happens. It will put a grin on your face every time!

Seeds remind us that every living thing has its own cycle of life contributing to the ecosystem, large and small. We must treat them with respect, nurturing them and conserving them. It's a matter of sustainability and survival.

To do this successfully, you need to know all about seeds. That's where we swoop in, offering you all the tools you need to start seeds, ensuring that they thrive and grow into beautiful and mature plants. We're going to answer your questions about everything from grow lights and viability to containers and planting media. We'll tackle issues such as damping off and overwatering, and

7

talk about the proper methods for hardening off transplants and planting them in your garden. We won't stop at addressing starting seeds indoors—we'll also give you the information you need to direct sow seeds straight into your garden. Then we'll delve deeply into how you can collect and save seeds for the future, so that you can continue the cycle.

We've added some detailed charts to give you specific information about seed starting on the prairies. As we all know, most of those lists you see on social media aren't particularly useful for gardeners in our region. And we've included several plant lists to help you decide what selections will work best in certain situations and conditions.

One of the most exciting parts of gardening is that we're all constantly learning and experimenting. There are always variables and changing conditions that make things interesting. Whether you are a seasoned seed starter or a total newbie, our goal is to impart the knowledge and inspiration you need to enjoy success with your gardening endeavours. Growing plants is a lifelong venture—and we want you to love it as much as we do!—SHERYL NORMANDEAU & JANET MELROSE

What is a seed?

All flowering plants reproduce by seeds. When you look at a seed, no matter what its size, it appears inert in your hand. Although they are dormant, seeds are living organisms. Each contains an embryo and stored food to aid its journey into the light, encased in an aril or seed coat if they are angiosperms, or naked if they are gymnosperms. The seeds of angiosperms are found inside the ovaries. Herbaceous plants, grasses, shrubs, and most trees are angiosperms. The seeds of gymnosperms are not enclosed; they are found on leaf- or scale-like structures called megasporophylls. Use *that* at your next trivia night! Conifers are gymnosperms.[1]

Seeds come in many forms and, accordingly, go by many different names, including pips, stones, nuts, kernels, and pits. The largest seed in the world belongs to *Lodoicea maldivica*, a type of palm. The seed tops out at a whopping fifty-five pounds (twenty-five kilograms)! The smallest seeds are microscopic, weighing just ten-billionths of an ounce. They come from a type of tropical orchid.[2] **—SN & JM**

Seeds are unique and beautiful, and come in all shapes and sizes. These calendula seeds are curved and almost shell-like.

Let's Talk about Seeds

1

What is the difference between heirloom, heritage, and hybrid seeds?

Ever since our ancestors 10,000-odd years ago started collecting seeds from foraged plants to sow in the first forest gardens, we have been selectively breeding plants. We don't have to look far for confirmation of that, considering the range of *Brassica* vegetables—from kale to kohlrabi—which all derive from a single wild species.

Early breeding was a matter of saving seeds from those plants that had the best qualities at the time. These plants are known as open pollinators, as they either are self-pollinating or cross-pollinate via wind, water, insects, and animals. They are also "true to type," as they usually have the same appearance and characteristics as last year's plants. Unusual variations happen occasionally when a genetic mutation occurs, which will either survive or die out. If we are saving seeds, we

Heirloom 'Brandywine' tomatoes are prized for their taste and size. These will ripen to a beautiful red-pink colour.

may choose to not continue to cultivate those plants that are significantly different from their parents, though if they look interesting enough, we may decide to grow them on to see if they are an improvement or just different. It is through these variations, called rogues, that we build up diversity within species. A couple of years ago, I had a weird, oval, light orange pumpkin growing in a garden, but I grew it to maturity. When harvested, the flesh was distinctly spaghetti squash! We saved the seeds, but the progeny didn't breed "true to type," nor was it particularly tasty, so I didn't continue growing them on.

The bulk of seeds available to gardeners are open-pollinated. They are part of the public domain, collected and grown by gardeners and businesses alike. Some have been around for a very long time indeed and have fascinating stories or provenance.

Enter heritage or heirloom seeds. They are the same thing, with Europeans choosing to call them "heritage" and North Americans going with the term "heirloom." I interchange the words readily, given my own gardening heritage growing up in three different parts of the world.

Originally, heritage seeds were designated as those in existence prior to the First World War, when the industrialization of seeds started. Others use the Second World War or the early 1950s, when hybridization of seeds came to the forefront, as their baseline. Still others use fifty years or thirty years as their guide. Finally, there are other gardeners who say that, as with all heirlooms, living or not, if they have value to us there is no time frame required or limitation involved to be considered an heirloom seed.

In many instances, these seeds have developed defence mechanisms against local insects and pathogens. "Sustainable resistance" is developed through allowing our plants to tough it out against native organisms and thrive.[1] They have developed hardiness to the climate and weather extremes on the prairies.

Most heirloom seeds are valued for their superior texture and taste, unique shapes, colours and sizes, and fragrances. They also may have less resistance to pathogens and other pests. They may be less productive or may not mature at the same time. Not all heirloom seeds are great seeds, but we value them for their stories—just as I may have a dreadful heirloom in my living room that I would never give away, never mind hide, because it has been in the family for aeons. Somewhere, sometime, someone in the family is going to love it!

Hybrid seeds (F1) are bred for uniformity, ease of harvest, storability, bigger blooms and different colours, resistance to various diseases, and so forth. They are created by selecting qualities between varieties and manually cross-pollinating the two. The resulting seeds are hybrids as they have genes from different parents. Hybrid seeds are known as cultivars, as in a "cultivated variety," and the cultivar name is enclosed by single quote marks. For example, the widely popular Sungold tomato is *Solanum lycopersicum* 'Sungold'. But we never get anything for free, and attributes can be lost in the process, such as diminished taste or scent, tougher skins, decreased nutrient values, and viability of seed. Hybrid seeds are the property of the breeder and often trademarked, making it illegal to collect your own seed from hybridized plants. It is also impractical as hybridized seed rarely grows true to type from seed we collect.

Should we grow only open-pollinated seeds, heirloom, or go with hybrids? The decision is a personal one. It also can be practical if you are looking for certain qualities that only a hybrid can provide, such as early maturity in short frost-free zones. Or perhaps you love the appearance and taste of heirloom tomatoes. Open-pollinated seeds are generally less expensive than hybrids, which can be a consideration.

My choice is usually a mix of everything, depending on what I am growing and where, with a strong preference for open-pollinated seeds, heritage or not. However, if I do choose a hybrid, I do a bit of research because I want to know about the grower and if the seed has been trademarked before I lay out that extra cost. If I can find a similar open-pollinated one through my research, then I will usually go with that one instead.[2] —JM

What are organic seeds?

Organic seeds are those that have been harvested from plants grown using organic cultivation methods. Growers of seed for commercial sale must be certified organic by a regulatory body. In Canada, that task is undertaken by the Canadian Food Inspection Agency.

The fact that the seeds have been harvested from organic plants does not in any way influence how the plants will ultimately turn out—that's up to the genetics of the plants, and whatever external factors (weather, siting, soil, sunlight, water, nutrition, pests, diseases, and so on) facilitate or hinder their ability to thrive. You can plant organic seeds and then raise the plants non-organically, although if you're going to the extra expense of purchasing organic seeds, it probably follows that you'll want to raise the plants organically.—SN

The scarlet runner bean plants that these seeds were harvested from were grown organically.

What are genetically modified (GM) or genetically engineered (GE) seeds? Are they available to home gardeners in Canada?

Genetically modified or engineered seeds are a minefield, with information and misinformation abounding, wrapped up with individual people's values and beliefs.

In a sense, humans have been modifying the genes of plants throughout the aeons, through selective breeding of plants for desirable traits to serve many purposes, including better disease resistance, appearance, taste, nutritional content, and more. The development of hybrid seeds, using our evermore sophisticated knowledge and skills—not to mention technologies—allows us to do so more precisely and quickly. The US Department of Agriculture defines a GMO as "an organism produced through genetic modification," which covers a lot of ground.[3]

Genetic engineering, on the other hand, has a much stricter definition: "manipulation of an organism's genes by introducing, eliminating, or rearranging specific genes using the methods of modern molecular biology, particularly those techniques referred to as recombinant DNA."[4]

In the United States, a GE seed is one that contains DNA from at least two of the six different kingdoms—Animalia, Plantae, Eubacteria, Archaebacteria, Fungi, and Protista—which can be roughly categorized as plants, animals, and microorganisms. The engineering is done at the submolecular level by inserting DNA from one species into another. In other words, the seed would not have those characteristics without our intervention, as it would be outside of their usual biological or natural reproductive capacity.

Huge investments are required over a lengthy period to create, test, and market such seeds. Currently, only GE seeds can be obtained for large-scale crops, such as corn, canola, soybeans, and sugar beets, and these are available only to the agricultural industry, not to home gardeners. Other crops have been recently approved, such as the Arctic apple, which has been modified to reduce browning, and the Innate potato, which has been bred with genes from wild and cultivated varieties to reduce bruising. The Innate potato, because it has DNA from only one kingdom, is GM, but not GE. Likewise, the AquAdvantage salmon is an Atlantic salmon that has been modified with growth-hormone genes from Pacific chinook salmon and is GM.

Health Canada maintains a list of approved "novel foods" on its website that stretches back to 1994. However, just because it is on the list does not mean it is available commercially. One reason may be lack of market acceptance.

Currently, there are no GE horticultural seeds available in Canada, for the simple reason that none have been approved for sale by a federally regulated body. However, seeing as GE and GM seeds have gotten lumped together and are generally referred to as GMO, it is important to know the distinctions, if only to be able to navigate the literature, be informed, and—if it comes down to it—make choices that reflect your personal values.[5]—JM

What are the benefits of sourcing locally grown seeds?

As a matter of principle, we prefer to use locally sourced seeds for just about everything we grow—be it be annual flowers, vegetables, herbs, perennials, or wildflowers.

For some very sound reasons, we want to support people on the prairies, and Canadians, in general, who are saving seeds, either for their own use or for their businesses.

Gardening on the prairies is challenging, and never more so when we are growing species and varieties that are not native—which is often the majority of what we commonly grow in our gardens. Our native flora has evolved to be hardy for our conditions, including geography, soils, climate, and a host of other factors. When we grow other plants, collect their seeds, and then plant and grow them, they are incrementally adapting to our conditions. Whether it is flowers or food, the results are healthy plants that are thriving—not just surviving—with better productivity. Resiliency and resistance to native insects and pathogens comes as those that survive these challenges go on to produce seeds that are just that much better. If we have a choice of the same variety of seeds grown as close as can be to where we live versus seeds from another part of Canada, the States, or overseas, you can bet we will be going for local!

By encouraging local seed growers and seed savers, as well as federal research institutions, we are also contributing to greater genetic diversity and the development of new varieties. A terrific example is the work that Canada has done for over one hundred years to develop tomatoes that can handle our climate and mature before winter freezes them solid. At the turn of the twentieth century, Canadians didn't grow tomatoes very often. They simply took too long to mature, and a species that is native to Central America didn't like our climate. Enter the Central Experimental Farm in Ottawa, established in 1886 as a research institution to promote Canadian agriculture. While much of their early work was focused on developing wheat varieties, an assistant researcher, William T. Macoun, started work on tomatoes. The 'Alacrity' tomato was introduced in 1916 and was our first Canadian-bred tomato. Over the decades, many more were developed at various agricultural stations, including ones in Morden, Manitoba, and Beaverlodge, Alberta. The work still goes on today at the Vineland Research and Innovation Centre in Lincoln, Ontario, and in many home gardens. Who wouldn't go for 'Manitoba', 'Sub Arctic Plenty', or 'Canada's Pride'?

Lastly, but just as importantly, by sourcing our seeds locally, we are tapping into and building our communities of seed savers. What could be more worthwhile?[6] —JM

Those packages of wildflower mixes you can buy in the stores: Are they good to plant in our area?

Over the years, I have been given many a container or seed packet of wildflower mixes, including the now (in)famous Cheerios honeybee mix. I always hesitate to use them, and they usually sit in my seed drawer until they are dust.

There are many reasons for my reluctance.

Wildflower is such a loaded word with many nuances. To many gardeners, me included, it means species native to a geographic area. To many, it also means annual flowers, but many wildflowers are perennial in nature, and some are biennial where they are native but may be only annual in our climate. Then there are conditions needed for them to grow, including the amount of sunlight, the type of soil, and the moisture levels. Are the species inside the packet even suitable to grow where we garden? Will they survive our summers—never mind the winters—if they are perennial? Will the species inside be recognized by visiting insects as nectar sources?

If you wish to purchase or are given wildflower seeds, the first thing to do is check to see whether the seeds are listed by their botanical name and (if appropriate) their variety. If only common names are provided, that is a red flag. Many species are known by the same common name but can be vastly different. I have seen mixes with hybrid seeds and named cultivars that are not wildflowers at all. If the seeds are in a container, look for how much by volume is seeds and how much is filler to make it look bigger. (I once was given a pretty container, eight inches [twenty centimetres] tall and four inches [ten centimetres] across, with just 500 seeds inside together with a lot of filler.) Is the mix prepared by a reputable company that is known for the purity of its seed mixes? Many tests have been done on wildflower mixes, and some contain weed seeds, some of which are noxious.

The next step is to determine whether the species in the mix are suitable for your area. Check the invasive-plant lists for your province, as the lists vary from province to province.

Then determine if your garden conditions will be ideal for the species in the mix. Just as important is how the species will behave in your garden. Some wildflowers are well-behaved in their native habitat but in rich garden soil can be extremely aggressive. Common yarrow (*Achillea millefolium*) forms tough mats that, once established, are extremely difficult to remove. A point to remember, too, is that most annual wildflowers are prolific self-sowers. Will their progeny be welcome in your garden for years to come?

My preference for wildflower mixes is to source them locally, where the people involved are experts and can help me select what is best for my garden. I may buy one of their mixes, but more often I will buy individual species, so that I can tailor the plants to what I like best and what will grow best in my garden. I'll go further, if the native wildflowers that I am looking for are biennial or perennial in nature. I'll buy them as plugs rather than seeds, since germinating wildflowers can be tricky, requiring similar soil conditions as in their native habitats. I've found that they are easier to establish in my garden as seedlings.[7] —JM

What do seeds need to germinate?

There is something that no gardener ever tires of watching and marvelling over. It's the process of a seed germinating—from the first little radicle root appearing from the seed that angles down into the soil, accompanied by the unfurling of the stem and cotyledon leaves as it emerges from the soil to start photosynthesizing.

In a nutshell, seeds require three things to be present for germination to be successful: water, the appropriate temperature in the growing medium and surrounding air, and oxygen. There can be other conditions for certain seeds, such as high heat as in fire, or the presence or absence of light, but these are specific to certain species.

The first step is inhibition, when the presence of water allows a seed to absorb moisture, which rehydrates the seed's cells. The seed coat is softened, and the radicle root emerges to form the primary root. It will immediately start to develop minuscule root hairs, allowing the seed to absorb water, oxygen, and the nutrients present in the growing medium. The seed will then increase respiration and metabolize the stored food contained in the seed. After cells start to divide, the embryonic stem will unfurl, dragging the cotyledon leaves up and above the soil surface.

Sowing seeds in soil too deep or too shallow, in soil that is waterlogged or too dry, or too cold or too hot will either prevent germination of all the seeds that have been planted or create conditions for spotty germination and weakened sprouts that will face an uphill battle to establish properly.

It is also important to know the optimum range of days each species will take to complete germination and to be visible. Some will emerge from the soil in three or four days, where others might take up to three weeks to do so. An uninformed gardener might give up, start all over, and end up uprooting slower seeds.[8]—JM

Are my older seeds good to sow?

Presprouting your seeds is an easy way to determine if they are still viable.

A seed is living: a capsule containing a plant embryo and the food that it will need to sustain itself through germination and sprouting until the photosynthesis process occurs. Seeds are dormant, but are still respiring and using up their food stores as they sit in your seed drawer. Some will be viable (able to germinate under the appropriate conditions) for years, and others will no longer be viable after a year. The growing conditions of the plants the seeds were harvested from and the maturation and storage conditions of the seeds are all variables to consider with older seeds.

Gardeners hate sowing seeds only to find that they don't germinate. To eliminate seed viability as a variable for seeds not germinating properly, a simple test will give you confidence that your seeds are good.

Place a moistened paper towel on a tray and place ten seeds on it. Cover it with another moist paper towel, and place it where it will get a little bottom warmth. The top of the fridge works best for us, but it can even be a countertop. Make sure to keep the paper towels moist. Then wait for the seeds to germinate in the usual range of germination time for each species.

If eight to ten seeds germinate, you have great viability, but even five out of ten seeds does not mean that all is lost. When sowing, double up on the seeds you are placing in each hole, and if both grow, cull out the weakest. Fewer than three seeds germinating are not worth the trouble. As well, it is important to know the normal viability of a species. Some species have seeds with close to 100 percent viability, while others have significantly less viability on average and what you may think are duds could be a reason to celebrate!

The bonus with this test can be that you have seeds that are already on their way to becoming seedlings, so use the ones that are germinating when you sow the rest in your packet. —JM & SN

What is a float test and can it determine the viability of seeds?

Although commonly used, the so-called float test is not considered consistently accurate. In our experience, the paper towel method (see pages 23–24) is much more reliable. However, if you wish to try it, this test is best attempted with wet seeds. (Dry ones can prove difficult test subjects since many dry seeds will naturally float. It doesn't mean that they are not viable; it's simply that they are not very dense.)

Ferment your wet seeds before performing the float test. If you don't, the gelatinous amniotic sac that coats the seeds will give you a "floating" result, and you'll think that all your seeds are bad. Fermenting the seeds will get rid of that sac.

Plop the seeds into a Mason jar, and add just enough water to cover them. Seal the jar, and shake it vigorously. Then remove the lid, and add more water. It doesn't matter how much you add. Just make sure you have enough headspace in the jar, so that you can clearly eyeball the waterline and spot if there are any floating seeds. Reseal the jar, and shake it again. Allow the contents to settle. The seeds that have sunk are good to sow; the floaters may not germinate as they should.[9] It doesn't necessarily mean that you should throw them out. If they aren't obviously deformed, discoloured, or broken, you may wish to try sowing them anyway, with the understanding that you may not have success with them.

You can also perform the test by placing the seeds in the jar and covering them generously with water. Allow the mixture to sit for fifteen minutes, then search for floaters.—SN

Seed viability

Curious how long you can keep those saved seeds and still get a decent germination rate? Here are some handy charts of some plants commonly grown on the prairies. Remember, these numbers are guidelines, and definitely not written in stone. (I know for a fact that I've kept several types of seeds for years well beyond the "best before" dates and had excellent germination rates—and there are also those stories about seeds found in musty attics and ancient tombs that have germinated in modern times without any difficulty.) But it goes without saying that properly stored seeds should have a longer viability than those that have not been kept well, and your best bet for success is to plant seeds within a year of collecting.

Sweet pea seeds should remain viable for a minimum of two to three years (or longer, if they are stored properly).

VEGETABLES

Seeds from crops in the Brassicaceae family (for example: broccoli, cabbage, kale, kohlrabi, Brussels sprouts, arugula, and cauliflower) will usually remain viable for three to five years.

Those from *Allium* crops (onions, leeks, and chives) will generally be viable for one to two years.[10]—**SN**

CROP	YEARS VIABLE
Bean	3
Beet	4
Carrot	3
Celery	5
Chard	4
Corn	1–3
Cucumbers	5
Lettuce	5–6
Peas	3
Peppers	2–4
Pumpkin	4
Radishes	5
Spinach	3–5
Summer and winter squashes	4–5
Tomatoes	3–7

FLOWERS

CROP	YEARS VIABLE
Alyssum	3–5
Amaranth	4–5
Calendula	5–6
Columbine	1–2
Cosmos	3–4
Dusty miller	3–5
Echinacea	4
Foxglove	2
Hollyhock	2–3
Impatiens	2
Larkspur	1–3
Lobelia	4
Lupine	3–5
Marigold	2–3
Nasturtium	5–7
Nicotiana	4–5
Pansy	2
Stock	4–5
Sunflower	3–5
Sweet pea	2–3
Zinnia	5–6

HERBS

CROP	YEARS VIABLE
Basil	5
Borage	1–4
Catnip	3
Chamomile	4
Cilantro	5
Dill	5
Lemon balm	1–4
Lovage	1–3
Oregano	1
Parsley	1–3
Thyme	1–4

When buying seeds, I notice that some of the packages say the seeds have been "treated." Treated with what?

Seeds may be treated with a variety of chemicals, processes (such as heat), and dressings, applied to—hopefully—increase the success rate of germination and growth, as well as to prevent the seeds from rotting in wet soil. Treatments may be antibacterial or antifungal. Although uncommon in seeds sold to home gardeners, seed treatments may contain insecticides. (You'll see this primarily in agricultural crops.)

If properly stored and not subjected to moisture, treated seeds may remain viable over longer periods in comparison to untreated seeds. Proponents of treated seeds find that there is no need to add separate fungicides and other chemicals to growing plants—the controls are already built in. Those who garden without the use of chemicals will want to carefully research any treatments their seeds may have undergone before they were packaged.

Reputable seed companies will be completely transparent about whether their seeds have been treated.

When handling chemically treated seeds, be sure to wear gloves (and wash them afterward to remove any residues).—SN

I am sowing extremely fine seed—it is almost like powder. Can I do anything to make distribution easier?

You have several options to successfully deal with very fine seed. One solution is to mix the seed with fine sand, which is available at some garden centres, craft supply stores, and even pet stores. (Check the area where the gravel and other aquarium substrates are kept.) Some gardeners mix fine seed with confectioner's sugar or flour, and I've even read about the use of coloured gelatin powder. The benefit of these methods is that you can see the trail of lighter-coloured material when you sprinkle the seed on top of the growing medium.

Seeds that are a little more substantial than powder may be sown with store-bought sowing tools. Dial types are common and possess more than one hopper to accommodate multiple sizes of seeds. If you do an inventory of your kitchen, you might come across an old, unused salt shaker that might work for certain sizes of seeds. Something else that is workable, if not ideal: save an old greeting card and place the seed inside the fold, gently tipping the card along the crease, so that the seed spills out onto the growing medium. It's tricky to spread the seed evenly with this method, however. A better option that guarantees proper spacing is to use seed tape—either some you've made yourself or from packages you've purchased (see page 31). Finally, if you have the patience, you can sow fine seeds by picking up each individual seed with the tip of a damp toothpick or wooden skewer and carefully positioning it on the surface of the growing medium.

Gently press fine seeds into the medium's surface. Don't poke the individual seeds in too deeply; they will be just fine as long as they have contact with the growing medium. And be super careful when you water! Watering from the bottom will ensure your seeds don't dislodge and float off into the edges of the container. When direct sowing, some gardeners will place a piece of row cover fabric or wood overtop of fine seeds to prevent them from rinsing off in a rainstorm. Remove the covering as soon as you see small dots of green popping out of the soil.—SN

If you have trouble spacing small, fine seeds, seed tape may be a good solution for you.

Capsule seeds may be composed of one type of plant seed or a combination of different ones.

What is seed tape? What are the benefits of using it?

Seed tape is pretty much as the name suggests: it's a roll of fully biodegradable paper "tape," embedded with seeds.

The seeds are perfectly spaced, according to the recommendations for that specific plant. Seed tapes are very useful if you wish to sow fine seed, such as carrots—it takes all the difficulty out of that task, as you simply dig your furrow in the soil, unroll the tape, and place it in the prepared ground. (Some seeds will need a light covering of soil; others won't.) Seed tape reduces the need to thin seedlings, which can be a time-consuming task that some gardeners dislike.

If you follow gardening sites on social media, you've likely seen instructions for how to make your own seed tape—it's an easy process involving a roll of toilet paper and a slurry of glue, made from flour and water. Use an artist's paintbrush to glue the seeds onto the paper—make sure you check the seed package for the recommended spacing!—and when your tape is dry, roll up the toilet paper on the tube and label it. You're ready for sowing! Bear in mind that if you're using nice plush toilet tissue, it won't break down in your soil as rapidly as the thin stuff will.

As an aside, another interesting product you may be seeing in the seed racks is capsule seeds. These are seeds—sometimes of one plant variety, sometimes of mixed plants—encased in a gelatin capsule, looking for all the world like a really large vitamin pill. The capsule also contains a hydrolyzed fish protein and honey. Are they easy to sow? Absolutely. Do your seeds need honey and fish protein? Certainly not to germinate. After the plants have developed beyond the first set of true leaves, you can begin fertilizing them, but it's not necessary before then. As for the honey, it's just there to act as a binding agent. Are the capsules fun? Sure! Are they worth the money? In my opinion, no, but I'll leave it up to you to decide if you want to part with your dough this way.—SN

What are pelleted seeds? Do they germinate better than non-pelleted seed?

Pelleted seeds are simply seeds that have been coated with an inert biodegradable material, such as clay, to make them bigger and/or more uniform in size, so that they are easier to sow, especially by those using mechanical seeders.

Lately, seed companies have been preparing seeds for faster germination, especially those with long germination times. The seeds are put in contact with moisture, then dried, and finally coated. Material used can include minerals and other ingredients designed to assist with good germination, with some even including oxygen-producing chemicals. Some seeds are also coated with graphite, so that they don't clump together as easily.

Candidates for pelleted seed are tiny ones in the carrot family, such as lettuce, parsnips, and parsley. Additionally, onion seeds are often available pelleted with graphite. With increasing demand, the range of pelleted seeds is expanding to include multigerm seeds, such as beets and chard.

Pelleted seeds come in bright colours, which used to put me off using them. Bright green, pink, blue, and silver seeds just don't seem right somehow, but, undeniably, it makes them easier to see as you sow them down the rows or in blocks. The other benefit is that you tend not to use as many seeds since they are easier to space. The temptation to sprinkle a few more for good luck is much reduced!

A downside of using pelleted seeds is that they are more expensive as you are paying for the extra processing involved. Also, pelleted seeds do not stay viable as long as they do in their "raw" state, meaning that any purchased seeds should be used within the current growing season. Exposure to humidity, light, and air in any form will start the germination process, degrading the seeds' vigour as well.

If you are using pelleted seeds, you can sow them in colder, wetter soils since they are meant to be able to germinate in less than ideal conditions. However, if you are sowing them in drier and warmer conditions, you must keep the soil moister than usual. If the soil is too dry, the coating will leach moisture from the seeds.

In the end, I recommend weighing the pros and cons before making a decision. Why not try both pelleted and non-pelleted seeds, and see how the results stack up?[11] —JM

These parsley seeds have been pelleted. The bright colour makes them easier to sow.

*Each of these little lumps
contains multiple seeds.*

My beet seeds look weird!

Beets and Swiss chard are common examples of plants grown from multigerm seeds. Instead of individual seeds, you actually plant a small lumpy fruit containing a cluster of seeds (usually up to five). This means you will always have to thin beet and Swiss chard seedlings, unless you plant monogerm seed types, of which there are a few.[12]—**SN**

Why are seeds dormant?

Birds can break hard seed coats and facilitate the germination of seeds.

When seeds are dormant, they cannot germinate. It is a survival mechanism, meant to prevent seeds from germinating when they might be harmed by poor weather or other conditions. There are several types of dormancies, but the two most relevant to prairie gardeners are exogenous and endogenous. Exogenous dormancy happens due to physical factors outside of the seed's embryo, such as a hard seed coat. Seeds can't germinate when moisture isn't able to reach the embryo and spur on germination.

Endogenous dormancy happens due to physiological or morphophysiological conditions inside the seed's embryo. For example, the seed's embryo may have physiological reactions to temperature or light, which may cause a seed to go dormant.[13] — SN

What does it mean to scarify seeds?
How do you do it?

Many seeds have hard arils or seed coats that require being degraded or abraded to break dormancy. The goal is to avoid germination at the wrong time of the year, so these seeds need to be scarred or scarified.

Some seeds with hard shells, especially fruit, require being eaten by birds or other animals. The acids in the digestion process will do the trick. Ever wonder why cotoneaster, mountain ash, and even strawberries start sprouting in the weirdest places?

Other seeds with thicker coats need exposure to water to soften their coats enough to open them. Seeds in the desert often need that sudden flood or burst of rain to trigger germination. Still others need fire to split open their coats, with Jack pine cones being a perfect example.

Thick but not really hard coats can be scarified by soaking them in water for up to twenty-four hours. Some advocate using hot water, but I usually use tepid water. The seeds will really swell and imbibe a lot of water, so a rough ratio of two times the volume of seeds is a good rule of thumb to follow. A perfect example of seeds that respond well to this treatment is peas, especially sweet peas. Others, such as nasturtiums, need a stronger treatment as their shells are harder. A cider vinegar solution (one part vinegar to four parts water) will mimic the process of digestion.

Manual abrasion can be employed for the very hardest seeds, but you have to be careful not to damage the embryo inside. Placing seeds in coarse sand and rolling them around in it for a while will often work. Alternatively, rubbing the seeds between sandpaper with just enough force to dull the coats is a good option for morning glory, hollyhock, lupine, and other smaller, hard seeds. Using a rasp to nick the seed just where the point of growth is located works for larger seeds, such as ornamental beans, canna, and nasturtium, though I find it to be tedious, not to mention tricky. Obviously, I don't have the dexterity needed!

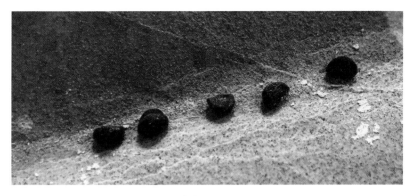

These morning glory seeds have been scarified with a piece of fine-grit sandpaper.

Immediately sow the seeds you have scarified, as they are now primed for germination.

As an aside, most vegetable seeds are softer and do not require scarification.[14] —JM

What does it mean to stratify seeds?

When you stratify seeds, you are using temperature (usually cold, sometimes a combination of cold then warm, depending on the species) to erode each individual seed's coat and promote germination. One other thing is necessary to properly stratify seeds: moisture. Remember, you're not storing these seeds for the long term—they don't need to be dry. You want to be able to sow these relatively soon. (The amount of time seeds should be stratified will differ from plant to plant, but four to five weeks is a general recommendation.)[15]

Wrapping the seeds in a damp (not sopping wet) paper towel and placing the towel in a sealed plastic or glass container in the fridge or freezer is one way to stratify seeds. Instead of a damp paper towel, you could also use a small plastic bag filled with vermiculite or fine horticultural sand.

A method that keeps making the rounds on the internet is to freeze the seeds in water in ice cube trays for two days, then thaw and plant straight away. It's a combination of soak and chill, which many gardeners swear by. I haven't personally done enough tests to confirm the efficacy of this method, but you should try it, if you want to.

No matter which method you choose, label your seeds! Unless you have an insanely good memory. (I don't!)[16]

One important thing to mention: the seeds of most annual plants (ornamentals and edibles alike) do not require stratification. You can choose to do it anyway, as it might hasten germination, but it's really not necessary. The seeds of some herbaceous perennials, trees, and shrubs are the ones that may need a little assistance.[17] —SN

Is there a general guideline for the planting depth for seeds? What happens if I sow seeds deeper than recommended?

It is advised that seeds be sown at a depth of twice the size of the diameter of the seeds. For example, large runner bean seeds that can be as large as your thumbnail can easily be planted at a depth of 2 inches (5 centimetres), but most other bean seeds should be planted no more than 1 inch (2.5 centimetres) deep. Smaller seeds, such as carrot, can literally be sown on the surface of the soil with a sifting of soil to cover them. Most seed packets specify the depth that you should sow the contents, but they can be overgenerous with their recommendations. If in doubt, sow a little shallower than deeper. No matter the depth, do make sure to gently pat down the soil covering your seeds to ensure good seed-to-soil contact.

Most people, including experienced gardeners, can be guilty of sowing seeds too deeply. On the prairies, I think we believe that if ¼ inch (6 millimetres) is recommended, to protect our seeds ½ inch (12 millimetres) deep must surely be better! The result though can be germination failure as the seeds may use up all their energy trying to get to the surface of the soil. If they make it, they can be weakened with poor growth as they develop. I once had someone ask me this question at a Seedy Saturday table, and I was just launching into a long science-based explanation when a small child beside me piped up with, "They die." Enough said!

On the other hand, if you plant seeds such as peas, beans, and corn, which should be sown ½ inch (12 millimetres) deep or more, too shallowly, they may end up being bird food or experiencing malformed development, such as their radicle roots ending up above the ground. Not a good scenario!

Most seeds do need to have some soil covering them, even tiny tomatoes. There are those that absolutely need light to germinate and should only be sown on the surface of the soil and gently pressed into the soil to attain necessary contact. Lettuce, dill, poppy, columbine, and cleome are just a few seeds that must have exposure to light to germinate.[18] —JM

Photodormancy: Light versus dark

Many seeds need only soil contact to germinate. Others exhibit photodormancy. This means that some seeds absolutely need darkness to germinate, while others must have exposure to light to break dormancy. The key is the pigment phytochrome, which regulates development processes. According to how seeds respond to this environmental factor, phytochrome will change form, in the presence or absence of light, and either suppress or trigger germination.

Those seeds that require light to germinate are typically tiny ones that are freely self-sown. However, they do not want to be germinating when there is too much competition for resources. So they will wait under cover of all the foliage around them until it diminishes enough for light to strike the seeds and the phytochrome to convert to the light form, triggering germination.

These are some of the species that require light to break dormancy:

* Columbine
* Gaillardia
* Lettuce
* Petunia
* Poppy
* Primrose

Seeds that require darkness to germinate will be dormant while on the surface of the soil and will only break dormancy when buried. This prevents premature germination for those species. When sowing these seeds in trays or pots, a trick to provide that necessary darkness is to cover them with a black garbage bag until germination occurs.

Some of the common species that require darkness to germinate include:

* Calendula
* Delphinium
* Pansy
* Periwinkle
* Phacelia[19]—**JM**

Don't cover poppy seeds
when sowing them; they
need light to germinate.

Should you fertilize newly planted seeds right away?

Seeds do not need fertilizer to germinate. The food they need to obtain enough energy to sprout their seed leaves (cotyledons) is contained in the seed itself. Once the seedling is past the cotyledon stage and is sporting its first couple of sets of true leaves, you should begin fertilizing. Some store-bought seed-starting mixes will have some fertilizer added, so there is no need to add more fertilizer right away. Hold off on the fertilizer until after you have transplanted your seedlings for the first time. If you're using soilless growing media, such as perlite, vermiculite, peat moss, coir, or a soil-based mix that does not contain fertilizer, you'll want to offer a diluted (about one-quarter strength) water-soluble balanced fertilizer such as 20-20-20 once a week. More is not better in the case of fertilizing—you can seriously harm or even kill your tender young seedlings with too much fertilizer. Go easy on them, and if you accidentally miss a week, that's okay . . . your babies will be fine.[20]—SN

These bean seedlings are still a bit too young to fertilize.

One of my tomatoes has done a really weird thing—the seeds inside the fruit have germinated, and there are sprouts popping through the skin. What is this?

It may look a bit gross, but vivipary isn't an indicator of some freaky mutation.

Cutting open a nice ripe tomato and seeing lots of little white growths inside can be quite startling! I have even had this happen to me with peppers, apples, and oranges, and it can occur with many fruits, including strawberry seeds sprouting on the outside of a berry.

This phenomenon is called vivipary, from the Latin, meaning "live birth." It really is premature germination that occurs when the hormone abscisic acid that governs seed dormancy runs out. If the conditions for germination are there after that, the seeds start to germinate.

Vivipary is most often found in fruit that has been kept in cold storage for a while; then when the fruit are taken out and are now sitting in a warm, possibly humid environment, germination begins. I have had vivipary happen with tomatoes that

I have grown at home, but that were left on the plant for too long. Other causes of vivipary can include too much nitrogen or not enough potassium while growing.

Although the fruit are edible, I find that the taste is a bit off for fresh eating, but the fruit are perfectly good for cooked dishes.

You can also just leave the sprouts to grow and plant them to see what happens. Many people have grown great tomato plants from these sprouts, but because they are hybrid seeds, they didn't look or taste anything like the original tomato.[21] —JM

This Swiss chard has gotten
a true jump on the season!

What is winter sowing?

It's as easy as turning an empty one-gallon (four-litre) milk jug into a miniature greenhouse! Then sow your selected seeds into premoistened potting soil, in the container. Park the container outside and wait until conditions are favourable for the seeds to germinate. The site must be out of direct sunlight (you don't want the seeds to pop up too quickly!) but exposed to snow or rainfall. There is usually no need to even water the jugs—nature will take care of that for you. A huge benefit of winter sowing is your seedlings do not require hardening off (see page 77), and it is easy to open the jugs to lift the block of soil out to transplant your young plants when the time is right. We love the ease of maintenance of this method—and, as a bonus, there is no need for grow lights!

On the prairies, you usually won't start your winter sowing too early. There's no need, as the seeds won't germinate in January anyway. In some areas, you also have to watch for chinooks—they can awaken the seeds a bit earlier than you want, only to be frozen with the next plunge in temperatures. Usually late February or March is a good time to plant most seeds for winter sowing.—SN

Indoor Growing

2

When should I start seeds indoors for transplanting later?

Peppers benefit from an early start indoors.

This short, simple list has been generated specifically for prairie gardeners and assumes that your first frost-free date is June 1. (If you're fortunate enough to live in a warmer region of the prairies, where you have an earlier frost-free date, you'll need to adjust accordingly.) And don't forget that it all depends on the cultivar as well. Check the dates on your seed packages and do the math. Remember that you need to factor in time to harden off your transplants before planting them in your garden.

VEGETABLES

* Early March: onions (seeds, not sets), leeks
* Mid- to end of March: peppers, tomatoes
* End of March: celery, eggplant
* Early April: artichoke
* Early to mid-May: cucumbers, pumpkin, squashes (except zucchini, which you can direct sow), watermelon

ANNUAL FLOWERS

* End of March to early April: petunia, snapdragon, verbena
* Early April: impatiens
* Early to mid-April: ageratum, castor bean, celosia, ornamental kale, thunbergia (black-eyed Susan vine)
* Mid-April: coleus

PERENNIAL FLOWERS

* Early February to mid-March: delphinium
* Late February to mid-March: sweet William
* Early March: lupine
* Early to mid-March: foxglove
* End of March to early April: hollyhock, rudbeckia (black-eyed Susan flower)[1] — SN

Bring on the blooms! Ageratum is a heat-loving, drought-tolerant annual that is easy to sow indoors for later transplant.

49

*Plastic cups are a suitable
option for starting seeds.*

What types of containers should I start seeds in?

Really, the sky is the limit when it comes to your choices . . . but there are a few things to keep in mind before you make your final selection.

Containers must be clean and free from chemicals, soil, and food. Wash them in hot, soapy water and rinse thoroughly.

Ensure your containers have drainage holes.

Start off with containers that are at least 3 inches (7.5 centimetres) deep.

Go ahead and raid the recycling bin. Yogourt cups, small plastic tubs and trays, and cardboard egg cartons are all fair game.

Many gardeners opt for plastic containers, but, as I've mentioned, paper and cardboard may be suitable as well. Other materials that work include terracotta, ceramic, wood, and glass. Metal is generally avoided as it can heat up significantly if placed in a sunny spot or under a grow light.

Seeding (propagation) trays with plastic cells, a clear plastic dome, and sometimes a capillary mat are ubiquitous because they work. As a bonus, they're not very expensive, and they're durable enough to reuse year after year. —SN

How can I make newspaper "pots" to start my seeds in? What about using toilet paper rolls?

Seed-starting containers on the cheap!

This method of making inexpensive containers for your seeds may not be around much longer as fewer people are subscribing to print newspapers, but if you have some in the recycling bin, this is a great project.

Canadian newspapers are printed with vegetable-based (usually soy) black inks, so there is no need to worry about leaching. (If you choose to use colour flyers or inserts, you may wish to call the publisher to allay any concerns.)

Grab a can of soup out of your pantry. If you make newspaper pots regularly and want a special template to use instead of food containers, you can purchase one from a garden centre. Resembling a staircase finial, they are usually made of plastic or wood.

Take two sheets of (folded) broadsheet newspaper and fold them in half lengthwise. You'll have a length of paper with four layers. Lay the can or template onto the paper, so that half of the container is sticking out of the paper—you'll want an allowance of several inches on the bottom. Roll the newspaper around the container, then fold up the open bottom snug against the base of the container. Think of it as a bit like wrapping a gift. You want to create a base for the pot that will not fall apart, so fold and crimp accordingly.

Remove the can or template, then fill your newspaper pot with soil. Set the newspaper pots into a plastic tray. Moisten—but do not soak—the soil. You're now ready to sow your seeds.

When it comes time to transplant, you can either carefully tear off the newspaper, or you can open up the base (so you don't choke the roots) and put the newspaper pot straight into your garden bed.

Even easier than making newspaper pots is to use toilet paper rolls. Cut them in half, then fold up one of the open ends to fashion a pot—you can cut slits in the roll to facilitate this, if you want—and fill with premoistened soil.

A word of caution if you use toilet paper roll or newspaper pots: be careful not to overwater, as mould likes to grow on wet paper.—**SN**

You always have these kicking around, so why not repurpose them?

What types of planting media should I start my seeds in? What is a soilless mix? What is a seed-starting mix?

We usually reach for a handy bag of "potting soil" when starting our seeds or planting our seedlings. Decades ago, potting soil did contain mineral soil, composed of sand, silt, or clay particles in varying proportions, but for various reasons, including weight, it is no longer a common ingredient in commercial mixes.

Seed-starting mixes are often just another name for soilless media, but the devil is in the details, as they say, as various ingredients can be added to either keep the cost low or make small bags rather expensive.

A good soilless medium for seeds absorbs moisture, air, and nutrients, and makes them readily available to develop plant roots. It should be loose and lightweight for good aeration so roots can readily grow and create a healthy root structure, but it should have enough heft to provide good anchorage and support as the plants grow. It ideally should have a neutral to slightly acidic pH, which favours good seed germination and early development. Finally, it should be free of weed seeds, pathogens, and soil toxins.

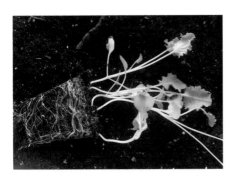

For their best chances at success, offer your seeds and seedlings high-quality growing media. For many gardeners, that means making it yourself!

The base of most media is either peat moss or coir fibre (the shredded hulls or fibre of coconuts). Their virtue is in their coarse texture and low pH, which enables good moisture retention. Perlite, a volcanic mineral heated to produce lightweight, white, popcorn-like particles, is often included. It provides for aeration, moisture retention, and drainage, all of which serve to ensure that the medium does not become anaerobic, which can rapidly cause seedling death. Vermiculite, which is mica superheated until it becomes light and spongy, is sometimes included, as it will hold many times its weight in water, but, on the whole, I find it holds too much moisture, and I avoid it in mixes if I can. Shredded bark is often added as a filler to a greater or lesser extent, but too much bark may cause nitrogen inhibition as the soil microbes will work to degrade the woody material, making nitrogen unavailable for the seedlings.

Some mixes will include a fine compost, either worm or regular compost, which adds nutrients for the seedlings and may cut back on the need to add supplemental nutrients. Other amendments can include mycorrhizal fungi, which promote root growth and plant health; dolomite limestone to ensure that the pH is not too low; and slow-release fertilizers.

Your seed-starting mix should have a fine texture and not contain noticeable woody material. Since it will be used strictly to germinate seeds and nurture them into their first growth, isn't necessary for the mix to contain a lot of nutrients. Once the seedlings are ready for pricking out or being potted into bigger pots where they will need additional nutrients, a switch to a regular mix can be made. Otherwise, supplemental nutrients will be required.

I judge a soilless mix by how fluffy it looks, but it should feel spongy with a nice texture to it. I want to see perlite, and preferably not really small granules, but bigger pieces and not so many that when the mix is watered, the perlite floats to the top, looking like it has snowed. If the mix has mycorrhizal fungi, I am happy, but I don't go out of my way to look for it. I also check to make sure there aren't many discernible pieces of wood and bark. I add to every mix a healthy amount of worm compost for those nutrients.

If I am making my own potting soil, I go with a balance of ½ premium sphagnum peat moss, ¼ perlite, and ¼ fine compost, and that extra trowel or two full of worm compost. Sometimes, I will also add a trowel of kelp meal or fish meal and a spoonful of mycorrhizal fungi. But it does vary according to what I am sowing and potting and what I have on hand, too. It is a bit like making a magic potion. You need to experiment to find out what you and your seeds like best. And that is half the fun![2] —JM

What are the benefits of using soil blocks? How do I make them?

Once you start using soil blocks, you may never want to go back to peat pellets or the ubiquitous cell packs with their small amount of room for soil and roots.

Soil blocks are simply blocks of soil formed to make free-standing cubes. The technique is European, but was made popular in North America by Eliot Coleman, an American organic gardening guru. A standard peat pellet, or the inverted cone or pyramid of a typical cell pack, does not really provide for enough volume of medium to promote good root development for seedlings. Underdeveloped root systems and root-bound or girdling roots can be common. The soil block is a cube, so automatically it has more volume—up to two-thirds more in some instances—even though its top may be no larger than that of a cell in a pack.

The real benefit though is how roots grow in a soil block. Instead of being cramped and circling around in a container, they go straight out till they reach the sides of the block, then are air-pruned. The entire mass of soil becomes filled with roots. To transplant, there is minimal disruption as you simply lift the block from the tray and place it into a prepared hole. No upending, squishing the sides of pots, or needing to spread roots out before planting.

Soil blocks are generally created using a soil blocker, which can be purchased at garden centres and specialty garden stores or online. A soil blocker is a handheld metal device that will create four or more blocks of growing medium for planting. You simply plunge the blocker into prepared growing medium, twist it a bit, and lift it out with the blocks full of growing medium. To remove them, you push the plunger, and the blocks of growing medium then slide out onto a seed tray, almost touching, but not quite. As each block of growing medium is ejected, a pin in the blocker even makes a dimple in each soil block, indicating where to place the seed. Blockers are well-designed, easy to use, and long-lasting.

Regular potting soil will not hold its shape for soil blocks. Eliot Coleman perfected a special formula that is the key to success when working with soil blocks. The recipe calls for premium-grade peat moss, which is fibrous and holds moisture well; coarse sand or perlite to provide air porosity; compost for nutrients (either worm compost or a fine high-quality compost, purchased or sifted from your own pile); and top-grade garden soil. Some additional elements are required, but in small quantities: lime to balance the acidity of the peat; optionally, blood meal or alfalfa meal for time-released nitrogen; colloidal phosphate for the roots; and either greensand or kelp meal for trace minerals. The ingredients are mixed together, and water is added, until the mixture looks like brown glop. A fun project, to be sure! —JM

A soil blocker in action!

Eliot Coleman's soil block recipe

3 parts brown peat
½ cup (64 grams) lime
2 parts coarse sand or perlite
3 cups (384 grams) base fertilizer
1 part soil
2 parts compost
Water, as needed

In a flat-bottomed container or wheelbarrow, add brown peat and lime. Mix. Then add coarse sand or perlite and base fertilizer. Combine. Add soil and compost, and do a final stir. Add water to make the mix wet, really wet.[3] —JM

Is it a good idea to start seeds in plantable peat pellets?

Peat pellets are inexpensive and easy to use, but they have some drawbacks to consider.

Peat pellets are ubiquitous at seed-starting time! Essentially designed to be a convenience for gardeners, they are composed of pressed peat or coir fibre wrapped in a fine mesh. They are easy to purchase and store; all you need to do to get started is to soak them in water, and the pellet expands to many times its depth, to about 2 inches (5 centimetres) tall and approximately 1 inch (2.5 centimetres) in diameter. The mesh encloses the peat, and you are good to go with putting seeds into the hole at the top. Pellets are promoted as a way to limit transplant shock as you are meant to simply plant the entire pellet—mesh and all. They are also promoted as a no-mess option. As always, we pay for the convenience as the cost is roughly three times that of purchasing a bag of potting soil and using trays and cell packs.

Despite the ease of using them, I find that peat pellets dry out quickly, requiring extra diligence to keep them at the correct moisture content. Additionally, when using peat pellets, seedlings have a rather small volume of medium for their roots to develop properly.

The other issue is that the mesh does not degrade in our soil. While it is made of biodegradable plastic, it is photodegradable, which means that in order to degrade, it must be exposed to light. The result is that the plant's roots remain constricted, which may lead to weak plant growth and overall poor health. I am always amazed at how small root systems can be when I dig up plants started in pellets. Plus, I find the mesh is intact, and the medium within the mesh is dry and hard.

Going the route of tearing off the mesh before transplanting negates the reason to use pellets as, to a greater or lesser extent, you damage the seedlings' roots. I do as a rule accept this damage whenever I encounter seedlings grown in pellets, even when it means I must remove all the surrounding soil if the plug or pellet has been potted into a larger pot. The resulting shock to the plant will be more readily overcome than having constricted roots throughout the growing season.

Ultimately, the choice to use peat pellets may come down to ease of use versus the mess of using loose mix, and whether you have the space for preparing the containers. —JM

The mesh that is used with peat pellets can constrict the root systems of plants.

Do I need to sterilize my soil before planting my seeds?

The short and quick answer is not at all. Soil—be it garden soil or potting soil—should be teeming with billions of organisms, and any sterilization process will kill them off. Secondly, the sterilization process, which is usually accomplished either by heat or by injecting steam, may change some of the matter in the soil. In the case of perlite and soluble salts, this may create conditions of phytotoxicity, which can inhibit germination and interfere with seedling development. Thirdly, the process becomes moot the moment it is finished unless the medium is packaged and kept under sterile conditions. Assuming that is the case, when you open the container it is no longer sterile, so the money spent on sterilized potting soil is wasted. You can sterilize soil or soilless media yourself, but it takes time and energy, and it smells awful.

What we do need is seeding medium that is free from weed seeds and pathogens, such as the 600-odd species of fungi known as "damping off." What that comes down to for me is always using fresh soilless medium for seed starting indoors, either from a supplier I trust or by making my own. Plus, all containers I use are cleaned with soapy water, so that I start off with a sanitized environment.

Practising good cultivation techniques for growing seeds indoors will go a long way to preventing pathogens from setting up shop. Keeping consistent air temperatures, ensuring the medium is moist but not wet, providing airflow, and always monitoring for signs or symptoms of disease are usually the most effective way to raise a crop of healthy seedlings.

Outside, in garden soil or in potting soil I am reusing after rejuvenating it with extra compost, those seeds are on their own. However, a three- or four-year crop rotation plan is a sound cultivation practice to reduce the potential for problems.[4]—JM

Is it necessary to use a heat mat when starting seeds?

No, it's not necessary at all to use a heat mat, but you can, if you want to. If you decide to use heat mats, bear in mind that not all seeds appreciate warm soils and, indeed, some will balk at germinating if you offer them supplemental heat. Others will germinate a bit quicker than they normally would when given a little extra warmth—it triggers feelings of "spring." If the room you grow your seeds in is really cold, using a heat mat may be useful for seeds that enjoy warmth to get going.

Heat mats are simple ways to supply some consistent bottom heat to your freshly sown seeds. The pads are usually made of several layers of plastic, containing an electrical heating element. The mats are fully waterproof. Some will have temperature regulators, but you don't have to fork over extra dough for that feature, unless you'd like to. Ensure all the electrical bits are in excellent working condition, and inspect for frayed cords or anything else that might pose a potential danger.

Use heat mats twenty-four hours a day until the seeds sprout. Once your seeds have germinated, remove the mats. You don't want to promote accelerated growth.[5]—SN

A heat mat can be a useful aid when starting seeds indoors.

Should I use a grow light for my seeds?
What types of set-ups are available?

As a general rule, yes, grow lights are highly recommended. While you can try to use the available sunlight that comes through your windows, chances are it is insufficient. In the winter, the days are short on the prairies, so if you're starting seeds, you'll likely need supplemental light. And be careful with southern exposures, as the light can be accompanied by too much heat.

Plants that are too far away from the lights will become etiolated (lanky and spindly, with a stretched stem). This act of "reaching for the sun" is called tropism, and the only way to prevent it is to provide more light.

Plants need a full range of the light spectrum—the whole ROYGBIV (red, orange, yellow, green, blue, indigo, violet)—to thrive and flourish. Each colour is a different wavelength, measured in nanometres.

Fluorescent lights are a common choice for grow lights. If you're "going with the fluor," you can purchase full-spectrum lights (or a combination of one cool spectrum and one warm spectrum) specifically for growing plants, but plain shop lights will work as well. Splurge and get new bulbs every year or two—you want these bad boys to be as bright as possible—since the light quality will diminish with use. (The discarded bulbs can be used in other areas of your home where the light doesn't need to be so bright.) There are more expensive—but brighter—options for fluorescent lights available: high output (HO) or very high output (VHO), but they require specialty fixtures.

LED (light-emitting diode) grow lights are available as full-spectrum (aim for the cooler end, if possible) or one-spectrum lights (red and blue are the most common, but other colours are available). If you're using single-spectrum lights, try to combine red and blue spectrum lights together for balance; this helps with the process of photosynthesis. The lights will degrade over a (relatively long) period of time and will need to be replaced periodically.

Compact fluorescent lamps (CFLs) are useful if you have an individual plant or a very small space that needs extra light; you can use the bulbs in a spotlight-style fixture, or even in a desk lamp. They are relatively inexpensive and can be used in standard fixtures that you may already own. Some gardeners use this style of light in small grow tents. There are several options for high-intensity discharge (HID) lighting. You can use metal halide lights (blue lights). These are perfect if you are growing seedlings and do not have any natural light at all. Metal halide lights are expensive to set up, as you need a special fixture to house them. High-pressure sodium (HPS) lights, made of sodium iodide gas, are another option, and they are available as full-spectrum lights, to boot. Ceramic metal halide lights are also on the market; they are more energy efficient than regular metal halide lights.

Other options for HID lighting include: dual arc bulbs, magnetic induction lighting, and light-emitting plasma bulbs. Some of these may be out of the price range of the average gardener, but they may be more economically viable in the future and as technology evolves.

Incandescent systems are tempting, due to the fact that the bulbs are super cheap, but here in Canada, we're trying to get away from these less environmentally friendly options. They are inefficient, burn out quickly, and are way too hot for growing plants. If you use these bulbs, your electricity bill will drastically increase.[6]

I'm hugely fond of the chain and S-hook mounts for grow lights, as this is the easiest way to maintain the proper distance between the lights and the seedlings as they grow. All you have to do is raise the chains. The lights should be 3 inches

For indoor growing, a good lighting system is important.

(7.5 centimetres) above the plants for two to three weeks, then the distance can be increased to 4 or 5 inches (10 to 13 centimetres). (This is so you don't accidentally burn your newly emerged seedlings.)[7] If you are using fluorescents and the fixtures are large, you may have to raise them a bit higher due to the heat they give off. Small fixtures won't produce as much heat. For the ultimate in convenience, you may want to look into countertop systems with built-in grow lights. They're pricey but attractive and perfect for year-round use.

The next question is: For how many hours per day should I leave my plants under the grow lights? It is recommended to give seedlings light for approximately fifteen to sixteen hours per day for the first couple of weeks, then you can decrease the time to between twelve and fourteen hours. It is generally accepted that ten hours is the bare minimum your plants can get by on.[8] —SN

Stretching in seedlings is an indicator that they do not have enough light.

Should I use a reflector hood with my grow lights?

If your lights generate a lot of heat, you won't want them too close to your seedlings—the recommendations for optimal light won't apply. Even if you're not worried about heat, you can boost the amount of light that gets to your seedlings by using a reflector hood. These hoods also help the light reach the lower parts of your plants, which are usually obscured by leaves.

Look for light fixtures that have built-in hoods. Some gardeners will place aluminum foil under their seed trays to reflect the sunlight or the grow lights back onto the plants. Materials such as Mylar and polymer can also work in the same way. These are commonly used with grow tents, but conditions can sometimes get too hot. Monitor your plants closely for signs of heat stress.—SN

Your seedlings should have robust, strong stems. These tomatoes are an example of healthy seedlings grown with the proper amount of light.

How long do I keep the dome cover (or plastic bags) on my seeding trays?

Too much condensation can lead to issues such as mould.

Once your seeds have sprouted, remove the dome or plastic bags. Keeping the cover on beyond that time facilitates sustained condensation and dampness, which can lead to mould and other problems. Of course, when you remove the cover, you'll have to carefully monitor how often you water because the trays will dry out more quickly in open air. Ah, the fun of striking that particular balance!—SN

Seedling Care

3

How should I water my seeds and seedlings so that they get consistent—but not too much—moisture?

Overwatering can prove disastrous—even fatal. Seeds and seedlings will rot in media that are waterlogged. Issues such as mould and damping off are encouraged when media are constantly wet. When it comes to gardening, mud is not the desired end goal of supplemental watering!

Underwatering is just as much of a problem. Seeds that dry out may not germinate well or may experience sudden death. Seedlings that are too dry may wilt and may not have the resources—such as an established root system—to recover. This means you need to focus on offering consistent moisture—but not huge glugs of drink.

When gardening indoors or in containers, the best option is to water from below. Fill shallow saucers partway with water and set your containers into the saucers for up to ten minutes. The water will be absorbed through the drainage holes in the containers. Remove any excess water that may be left in the saucers. Do not allow the containers to constantly sit in water, as the unrelenting dampness will only encourage mould. An excellent alternative is to use a propagator tray with a capillary mat.

If you are watering from above, a small watering can may be used. This is best reserved for seedlings, as it's too easy to dislodge seeds from their beds when watering this way. Do not splash water up into the foliage of the plants.

Now, to another burning question: How often should you water? The general recommended practice is to water your seeds and seedlings once a day, but there are a few factors that may influence the timing of this task. Container type, planting media, light conditions, soil and ambient temperature, and air circulation are all potential difference-makers. It's important to note as well that not all plants have the same water needs, and those needs may change depending on how large or mature your seedling is.

Poke a fingertip into the medium before you haul out the watering can. If you lift away a few crumbles of damp soil, then you can wait a bit longer to water.

If you're using tap water, it's a good idea to let it sit for at least twenty-four hours so that the chlorine in it can evaporate. Some gardeners choose to use distilled water to eliminate some of the salts that are found in tap water, but since your seedlings may be transplanted more than once, and may not be staying in their containers for too long (at least initially), you usually don't have to worry about salt building up in the soil.

Make sure that the temperature of the water you use is tepid. If you were drawing a bath, you wouldn't be too excited about the extremes of hot and cold, either.

If you've direct sown your seeds or transplanted starts into your outdoor garden, pretty much the same rules apply as indoors. Don't let your seedbeds dry out. Don't drown your seeds or plants. (That means not using what my former boss at the garden centre used to call the "firefighter's setting" on the hose nozzle.)

You'll often read about the "one inch" rule—that is, your plants need 1 inch (2.5 centimetres) of water per week. It's a generalization, and while it is workable as a guideline, it's a better idea to check the soil regularly and base your watering schedule on the needs of individual plants. Some parts of your garden may lie in full sun, while others are in shadier locales. Wind may be an issue in certain spots in your yard. These types of conditions will influence the rate at which your plants dry out.—SN

How can I ensure my seedlings have good air circulation around them?

Sufficient air circulation is important to the health of your young plants, helping to prevent problems such as damping off, rot, and mould. In addition, as plants photosynthesize, the stomata in the leaves of plants take up the carbon dioxide found in the air surrounding plant leaf margins. Movement helps to quickly replenish the supply of fresh air—and therefore, carbon dioxide—that plants can readily access in their immediate vicinity. Moving air also helps to eliminate excessive humidity on leaf surfaces, which can be a contributing factor to diseases. (These are just a couple of reasons why fans are so important in greenhouses.)[1] Another benefit: given suitable space and airflow, plant stems will tend to be stronger and less likely to become lanky. (You'll also have to ensure that they're getting the proper amount of light to nail that.)

Once they're transplanted outdoors, your plants will get all the fresh air they need, but while you've got them growing indoors, it's a good idea to use a small fan to gently blow air over the trays. (And I do mean gently—you really don't need much air movement at all. You don't want to accidentally break stems.) Place the fan adjacent to the trays, so that the air blows horizontally over the young plants. The fan should be pressed into service when the plants sport at least one set of true leaves. You don't have to run the fan all day, either. If you're able to use it for only an hour or two, that is better than nothing.

Bear in mind that you may need to adjust your watering schedule if you use the fan for long periods of time, as the soil or seed-starting medium may dry out more quickly due to the blowing air.

If you can't get your plants out into the garden until they have matured considerably, and the foliage is becoming dense and crowded, you can prune a few leaves to allow for more air exposure.—SN

How do I properly thin my seedlings?
What is "pricking out"?

Despite our best intentions, we always seem to end up sowing too many seeds, whether it is in cells, pots, or outdoors in the garden. Sometimes it is a shaky hand, or perhaps the wind blows them onto the soil, or more likely we believe that just a few more seeds for good luck will help things along nicely!

Naturally, the seeds all come up, and now we have the work of thinning them so that each will have the necessary space to develop properly and will have access to air, light, water, and nutrients. Failure to do so results in weak growth and seedlings that are prone to pests—whether it be a fungus or insects picking them off.

The best time to thin seedlings is when they have just grown their first set of true leaves and are no more than two or three inches (five to seven centimetres) tall. Prepare for the task by ensuring that the soil is moist, so that the small roots can be gently pulled out of the soil without damaging the remaining seedlings. Grasp each seedling by the leaves to remove.

These pretty little kale seedlings will need thinning soon.

You now have choices. You can either discard the seedling in the compost or leave it on the surface of the soil to quickly degrade. You can eat it, and I do love snacking while I am thinning!

Or you can increase your stock by potting on the thinned seedlings, which is called "pricking out." If you intend to prick out your excess seedlings, it pays to prepare ahead of time. Have cell packs or pots already filled with moist potting soil and create a hole in the middle of each one with a dibbler. Then, using a small tool—I use an old fork—gently lever out the seedlings, either one by one or in clumps. Hold each seedling by its leaves, never by the stem or roots, as they are very delicate at this point. Then, balancing the seedling on your dibbler, fork, or hand, place it in the prepared hole, so that its roots go down as far as possible. Firmly pat soil around the stem, and add a bit of water.

If you ended up being heavy-handed and the seedlings are in clumps, you can tease them apart by holding on to each set of leaves and gently pulling until the roots untangle. Success depends on you immediately transferring the seedlings to their new home as their roots will dry out quickly if left out for long. This technique works for just about all seedlings except for root crops like carrots. Even then, on occasion, I have gone ahead and pricked them out anyway. You never know your luck.

Another route to go—especially when dealing with seedlings that really hate to be disturbed at all—is to cut the extra seedlings right off at the base of their stems with small scissors. The roots will quickly degrade and contribute their nutrients to the remaining seedlings.[2]—JM

Why did my seedlings suddenly keel over and die?

In all likelihood, your seedlings are a victim of "damping off." This is a disease caused by fungi and oomycetes that are either seed- or soil-borne. It may kill planted seeds before they germinate or when they are at the seedling stage. Species of *Pythium* and *Phytophthora* are often the ones responsible for doing in seedlings and are appropriately called "water moulds" as their spores will swim through soil moisture, lashing two fine threads to propel themselves.

The organisms form colourless threads throughout the soil, and when they encounter a root or stem, a further microscopic thread emerges that penetrates the plant's cellular wall and disrupts normal cell function. Often the first symptoms of damping off are the stems of seedlings looking pinched or literally falling over where the stem emerges from the soil.

The only solution is to immediately dispose of the seedlings as there is little to do to save them, and there's a good chance that the fungi will spread via spores to other seedlings. There are fungicides available—mostly copper-based—but you really do not have a lot of time to act to prevent further trouble with the rest of your seedlings.

Prevention is really the key to avoiding damping off, and it starts with good hygiene and good cultivation practices. Do wash all your containers ahead of time, finishing off with a rinse in a diluted solution of three parts water to one part vinegar or undiluted 3 percent hydrogen peroxide. Always use fresh soilless medium.

When sowing, do not crowd the seeds, so that there will be good air circulation between the seedlings as they grow. If they are too crowded, thin them out. Practising an excellent watering technique is crucial (see pages 70–71) as the name damping off really says it all. The fungi love damp and waterlogged soil, and we do love to water our seedlings.

Avoid misting or splashing leaves with water as the fine droplets on leaves can be another entry point for spores.

Natural fungicides can also be used as a preventive measure. Both cinnamon and chamomile have fungicidal properties. A sprinkling of cinnamon on the surface of the soil can be effective, as can watering with a solution of weak chamomile tea, roughly 1 tea bag or 1 mounded teaspoon full of dried flowers for 4 cups of water. Or do as I do: brew your cup of tea for the night, then make your seedlings tea by reusing your tea bag or flowers with 3 cups of hot water, letting it sit overnight. Then everyone is calm!

Finally, do not be discouraged if you experience damping off. Almost every gardener has had at least one encounter with this challenge, and some hard-earned knowledge will come from it to prevent further outbreaks.[3] —JM

Why is hardening off so important when transplanting seedlings in the spring? How should I successfully go about it?

If you've ever been on a tropical vacation during one of our frigid prairie winters and returned home to find that you just can't seem to adjust to the shockingly cold temperatures and dry air, then you'll completely understand what happens to our lovingly pampered seedlings when you take them out of their indoor spa-like conditions and plop them into the harsh outdoors. They get grumpy. Sometimes they give up and keel over.

You need to go slow. The transitioning process you must take with your new plants is called "hardening off," and it's just what it sounds like: getting them ready for the hard, cold reality of life outdoors. Hardening off should take a minimum of one week. Two weeks is better. Work this time into your calculations for planting. Also, ensure that the weather is co-operating, and that it isn't too cold—just because you think it's time to plant doesn't mean Mother Nature agrees!

To harden off your plants, take them outside into a site that is out of direct sunlight and is sheltered from the wind, and allow them to sit there for a few hours a day. Bring them inside at night. Over the next week or two, offer them a bit more sunlight and a bit more exposure to the wind, and let them sit outside for a few more hours each day. By the end of one or two weeks, they should be ready to survive the conditions of their new home, and you can plant them outside.

One important thing to note: don't harden off your seedlings too soon. They need to be old enough, large enough, and strong enough before they are planted into their outdoor locations. Don't rush the process, as doing so can potentially harm the little guys. —SN

Sun scorch is a common problem when young plants are exposed to too much direct sunlight while hardening off.

When is the best time to transplant seedlings outdoors?

You've hardened off your baby plants and are ready to put them into the ground (or into containers outdoors). Choosing the optimum time to do the job will help your new seedlings get their best crack at survival. If you can tick off all the boxes in this checklist, you're good to go!

☐   Your long-range forecast doesn't advertise frost, snow, or several days of torrential downpours or blasting winds.

☐   The ambient temperature isn't too hot. If the thermometer is sitting at well over 70°F (20°C), choose a cooler time—but not too cool. Transplanting tomatoes at 40°F (5°C) may not kill the plants, but it won't promote happy plants, either. Finding the best ambient temperature may mean you have to wait another day or two to transplant—or it may simply mean that you have to plant in the morning instead of the afternoon.

☐   Your soil temperature isn't too cold. Most seedlings can't hack chilly soils. It's best to transplant warm-season crops when the soil temperature hovers around 60°F (15.5°C).[4]

☐   The day is on the overcast side.

☐   You have some cloches or covers on standby, just in case the weather takes a bad turn and your plants need shelter.—SN

Attempt to minimize transplant
shock by planting out your
seedlings when the temperatures
are cool (not cold) and the day
is overcast.

Cold frames can be extremely
useful in the prairie garden.

**Protect your green babies with
cloches or cold frames**

Cloches are small covers—usually
made of glass or plastic—that are
plopped overtop of individual plants
when weather conditions are not ideal.
Everything from a beautiful, classic bell
jar design to a milk jug with its bottom
cut open can serve as a cloche. Tent-
style cloches, fashioned from stakes
and heavyweight plastic or tarp, are
also effective.

Cold frames may be constructed of
aluminum or wood, often with rigid,
clear polycarbonate cladding. More
expensive models might use glass—
and if you're creative, you can upcycle
doors or windows to use when con-
structing one. Some cold frames are
lightweight and manoeuvrable, so you
can pick them up and position them
where needed; others are more per-
manent structures and may even have
a gravel or poured concrete base. The
cladding can be opened and closed,
according to ambient temperatures,
allowing young plants a chance to get
some sun on a warm spring day and
to cozy up during a cold night.—**SN**

Cloches offer cold protection
for individual or small
groupings of plants.

Direct Sowing

4

What are the best candidates for direct sowing into the garden?

Some plants just don't need a leg up, even in our ridiculously weird prairie climate. It may be because they have root systems that don't like to be moved around once they get going, or perhaps you don't want to worry about hardening them off and coping with transplant shock once you finally get your young plants out of the house. Rather than starting seeds indoors and transplanting them outside, some seeds are simply more amenable to being sown into the ground when the soil and ambient temperatures are ideal for planting. This is a very short list of a few seeds we like to direct sow.

VEGETABLES AND HERBS

* Basil
* Beans
* Beets
* Borage
* Broccoli
* Cabbage
* Calendula
* Carrots
* Cauliflower
* Chard
* Cilantro
* Corn
* Dill
* Kale
* Kohlrabi
* Lettuce
* Mint
* Parsley
* Parsnips
* Peas
* Radishes
* Scallions
* Spinach
* Tarragon
* Turnips
* Zucchini

ANNUAL FLOWERS

* Cosmos
* Marigold
* Nasturtium
* Nigella
* Poppy
* Sunflower
* Sweet pea
* Zinnia[1] —SN

*Peas grow quickly
and don't like being
transplanted, so it's best
to direct sow them.*

On seed packets, what does the term "days to maturity" or "days to harvest" mean?

This is an intriguing, not to mention loaded, question!

At its very simplest, "days to maturity" refers to the number of days, under ideal conditions, that the seeds will need before the plants are harvestable, be it their roots, leaves, fruit, or flowers.

Depending upon the source, "days to maturity" can include the days it takes for a seed to germinate, reach the true leaf stage when it can start photosynthesis, and progress to harvest or setting fruit. But more often, the clock starts ticking when the seed germinates and can be seen poking above the soil and ends with full production—be it roots, leaves, flowers, fruit, or mature seed. Should the seed packet include both "days to germination" and "days to maturity," then the seed source has separated the two timelines, which I prefer, given all the variables in play for germination itself.

Such information is important for decisions we make about what to plant, even down to the variety or cultivars we choose, given the average number of frost-free days that we experience across the prairies. No point in planting something that is going to take 150 days to get to maturity if on average where you live you are looking at only 100 such days!

The other important aspect of days to maturity is that this information is based on ideal growing conditions. Not too hot, not too cold, even soil moisture, humidity just right, no wildfire smoke, and so on. Weather conditions that are less than optimal will slow down plant growth and development, continually adding extra days before we can enjoy and/or harvest our plants.

Which all goes to say, when choosing what to sow, build in a nice allowance of time beyond what the seed packet says for your seeds to all grow to maturity without risking running out of days before the inevitable season-ending frosts may come. Because I have never witnessed that Shangri-La of the perfect growing season![2]—JM

What is bacteria inoculant used for?

A stable and inert gas, atmospheric nitrogen (N_2), forms roughly 80 percent of the air we breathe. The energy of a bolt of lightning works to convert atmospheric nitrogen to form nitrogen oxides (NOx). Together with oxygen (O_2) and water (H_2O), they go on to form nitric acids (HNO_3) and nitrates (NO_3.), both of which are utilized by plants.

Many life forms can also fix nitrogen, but it is bacteria that do much of the heavy lifting in this department. Some are anaerobic and some are aerobic; some are ocean- or freshwater-dwelling, and others are land-based.

Soil-dwelling bacteria, such as *Rhizobium* and *Frankia*, form symbiotic relationships with certain plant families and species by fixing or converting inorganic atmospheric nitrogen into organic ammonia nitrogen (NH_3), thereby making this essential element available to plants. It is then biosynthesized into more complex compounds, such as amino acids, proteins, and so forth.

As an example of mutualism, this relationship works when the bacteria enter the plant through its fine root hairs. Nodules—a specialized root tissue—grow where the bacteria convert the nitrogen that is present in the soil. In return, the plant supplies carbohydrates to the bacteria. Some plant species, such as alfalfa, can obtain all their nitrogen through this process. Others do so to a greater or a lesser extent, with a side benefit, making excess nitrogen available for other plants to use.

While, theoretically, nitrogen-fixing bacteria are always present in soils, it can get tricky when specific strains of bacteria are needed to match with certain host species. For example, the *Rhizobium* inoculant for alfalfa isn't going to work with fava beans. In both agriculture and gardening where the soil is being constantly cultivated and crops rotated, populations of the right strain of bacteria may not be present or in sufficient amounts. Using inoculant provides that guarantee that they will be, and the awesome symbiotic relationship will get to work for you and your crops.

An inoculant is nothing more than bacteria being held in either a black, peat-based powder or a liquid. It is active, but its populations will diminish over time, so check the expiry date on the package before you buy, and use it right away. Don't purchase it and save it until the following season. The inoculant should have been stored somewhere cool and without exposure to light, such as a refrigerator, for it to be viable.

Either apply it as a powder directly to the seeds, covering them well, or make a sludgy slurry with water and the inoculant. Drop the seeds in the container with the slurry, and let them get nicely coated, then sow immediately, so that the bacteria can get to work.

If you are curious, dig down around the roots of a few mature plants. If you see pinkish-red nodules on the roots, this is evidence of the process, up close and personal. Once the plants are dead, the nodules will go from a green to a tan to an almost cream colour, signifying that there isn't active fixing happening. Rather than dig up the roots and nodules, just till them back into the soil. Next year the bacteria will be there for a future crop to benefit from.[3] —JM

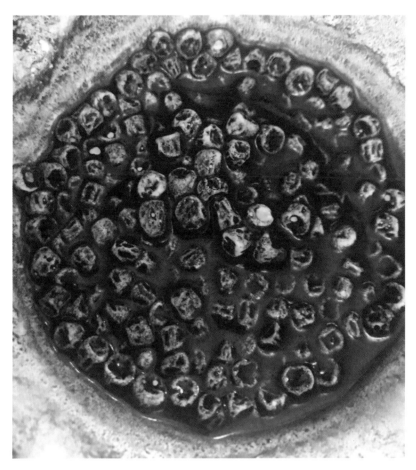

*These pea seeds have
been mixed with bacterial
inoculant in preparation
for planting.*

What are "frost-free days"? Why is it important to know about them?

Frost-free days for any given area refers to a statistical average over thirty years of the number of days that will likely not experience temperatures less than 32°F (0°C) at the coldest part of the day. It is not a guarantee that frost will not occur—it could still freeze if the conditions are right. The average number represents that time where plant growth should happen, uninterrupted by frost.

The chances of variation from the last date in spring to the earliest date in fall are around 30 percent, but given the weather extremes that are regularly experienced on the prairies, the number of frost-free days is more a guide than something to rely on. Over the past thirty years, I have seen heavy frost on June 10 and as early as August 25. In an area that now expects to have 112 to 114 frost-free days on average, if both those dates had happened in the same year, which thankfully they did not, there would have been only 74 frost-free days that year!

Topography and geographic location play a big role in whether your garden may or may not escape a late frost or experience an extra early frost, with those at higher elevations likely to have fewer frost-free days. A friend of mine not far out of Calgary but in the foothills and in a river valley has only 47 frost-free days on average! Even microclimates in your own garden can experience variable frost-free days.

Light frost is considered to be between 29 and 32°F (-2 to 0°C), where frost will kill tender plants such as tomatoes.

Moderate frost occurs between 25 and 28°F (-4 to -2°C) and will damage the foliage but not necessarily kill most plants.

Heavy frost occurs below 24°F (-4°C) and will kill or do heavy damage to just about every plant we typically grow.

Rule of thumb: use the number of frost-free days in your area as a guide to what you might be able to grow in any given season. Make wise choices, and then cross your fingers that it will all work out well. But don't be shocked if you are surprised with an unwelcome frost.[4]—JM

How do I keep birds and rodents from eating my newly sown seeds?

The best way to keep the seeds you have spent so much time sowing from becoming critter food is a physical barrier. At other stages of the season, other tricks to scare away marauders are needed, such as sprays that smell awful to them or glittery compact discs twinkling in the sun.

I use my go-to floating row cover and put it over the beds immediately after sowing, weighted down by rocks or old logs. The thin-spun polyester sheets are lightweight, assist in keeping soil evenly moist and warm, and boost the air temperature a bit higher. Most importantly, the row cover protects those seeds both from drying winds and from flying, hopping, and walking creatures. That includes pets doing their business in your nice bed, too. The row cover stays on while seeds are germinating and getting going as seedlings, and helps nurture the tiny seedlings into robust plants. I just loosen the row cover as the plant growth takes off.

I also use burlap sacks to cover the beds to assist in germination, especially with those seeds that have long germination times. The heavier burlap keeps soil moisture even, and slow crops like those in the carrot family often pop up days earlier. I check the seeds every day or so, and when I see them coming up, I take the burlap off, leaving the row cover to do its work.

An old trick my granddad used to use was to place planks over the rows until his seeds sprouted. The burlap is just a variation on that theme.

Just keep your seeds covered however you like to give them a better chance against the elements and hungry critters![5] —JM

Beans are not fond of the cold. Wait to sow them until the ambient and soil temperatures are balmy.

What are cool- and warm-season crops? Why is it useful to know the difference?

Whether you're direct sowing or transplanting starts of vegetable crops, it pays to know whether they are classified as "cool-season" or "warm-season" crops. This can help you decide when to plant. Cool-season crops are those that you want to plant first, as early in the season as you can, so that they are ready to harvest before summer temperatures cause them to lose quality or go to seed. If you are on the ball and the weather co-operates, you can plant cool-season crops again in the fall, but they need to have enough time to reach a harvestable size before heavy frosts hit.

As befits their name, warm-season crops need warm soil and ambient temperatures. If you plant them too soon, they may not germinate. These are crops that you may need to start indoors early or direct sow well after the last frost date.

COOL-SEASON CROPS

* Arugula
* Beets
* Broccoli
* Cabbage
* Carrots
* Cauliflower
* Chard
* Collards
* Kale
* Kohlrabi
* Lettuce
* Parsnips
* Radishes
* Spinach

WARM-SEASON CROPS

* Beans
* Corn
* Cucumbers
* Eggplant
* Peppers
* Pumpkin
* Summer squashes
* Tomatoes[6] —SN

Why is the temperature of the soil so critical to seed sowing?

Seeds are kind of like Goldilocks in that familiar fairy tale with the three bears: they need their porridge (I mean soil temperatures) to be just right before they germinate. Too hot or too cold, and they either do nothing at all, or they take forever to show up. Most seeds prefer a germination soil temperature range of 65 to 80°F (18 to 26°C), so aim for that, but remember that many will germinate when it's much cooler. Take a look at these soil temperature charts, and time your sowing accordingly.

VEGETABLES

CROP	GERMINATION TEMP. RANGE (MINIMUM TO MAXIMUM) °F/°C
Beans	60–85/15–29
Beets	40–85/4–29
Cabbage	40–95/4–35
Carrots	40–85/4–29
Cauliflower	40–85/4–29
Celery	40–70/4–21
Chard	40–85/4–29
Cucumbers	60–95/15–35
Kale	40–85/4–29
Kohlrabi	40–95/4–35
Lettuce	40–90/4–32
Onions	50–95/10–35
Parsley	50–85/10–29
Peas	40–75/4–23
Peppers	65–95/18–35
Spinach	40–75/4–23
Squashes	60–95/15–35
Tomatoes	50–95/10–35

ANNUAL FLOWERS

CROP	GERMINATION TEMP. RANGE (MINIMUM TO MAXIMUM) °F/°C
Coleus	70–75/21–23
Cosmos	70/21
Geranium	70–75/21–23
Impatiens	70–75/21–23
Nasturtium	65–70/18–21
Nicotiana	70–75/21–23
Petunia	75/23
Portulaca	75/23
Sunflower	70/21
Zinnia	70/21

If you're like me and you love gadgets, you can purchase a soil thermometer to test the soil and make sure it's ready for seeding. Ensure you check several areas of your garden bed, not just one spot, as some areas may be colder than others.

A final important thing to remember: the optimal range of soil temperatures for plant germination is not necessarily the same as the optimal range of temperatures that the plants themselves will grow and flourish in.[7]—**SN**

Soil temperature is an important factor in successful seed germination. A tool such as this thermometer can help you decide when it is time to direct sow your seeds outdoors.

What are the best plants to sow in the fall?

Try sowing a few spinach seeds in the fall to give yourself an early crop the following spring.

Sowing seeds in the fall for an early start to spring planting is a marvellous way to wrap up the gardening season!

Many seeds that require stratification — breaking dormancy to promote germination — can be sown directly into prepared beds or into containers that are then placed into a trench and mulched over for winter. Many native plant seeds and common herbaceous perennials require a long period of stratification and are best propagated by fall sowing.

A surprising number of our commonly grown edibles will survive the rigours of winter and reward us with early germination once the soil temperature is right for them. Avoid seeds that require warm soil temperatures to germinate as they will usually rot in the cold, wet soil of spring, but do sow those cool-season edibles that have an optimal germination range of soil temperatures from 34 to 42°F (2 to 6°C). The trick is to wait until the soil has cooled down below 32°F (0°C), preferably after a frost or an early snowfall that has melted; prepare the bed as you normally would in the spring with a smooth soil surface; sow at the correct depth; and allow for a percentage of seeds that may not make it.

After sowing, do not water them, but do cover the bed with a layer of well-anchored floating row cover. The cover will help prevent soil erosion over the coming months. If you are in chinook territory, an additional cover that is easy to remove come March is beneficial to prevent excessive loss of moisture during warm spells. I have used burlap sacks to great effect. Success is not always guaranteed, but when it works it really is worth doing!

From first-hand experience, here are some edibles to try for short-season gardening that will have the promise of goodly harvests:

- Arugula
- Chard
- Endive
- Kale
- Leeks
- Lettuce
- Onions
- Peas
- Radishes
- Spinach
- Turnips

Garlic is technically not a seed as it is propagated mostly by cloves, but absolutely plant it in the fall, if you can, especially in shorter growing season areas.[8] —JM

Collecting Seeds

5

When saving seeds, collect them from plants that have the characteristics that you desire.

What kinds of positive traits should I select seeds for?

Saving seed isn't just a matter of collecting whatever your plants produce; you want to be a bit more thoughtful about the process than that. The seeds you collect now represent future generations, so select seeds from plants that exhibit the characteristics you want. The kinds of traits you're looking for may include:

* Vigour
* Early production
* Drought tolerance
* Stockiness
* Hardiness
* Bolt resistance
* Crack resistance (fruit)
* Disease or insect resistance
* Colour (flowers, foliage, fruit)
* Flavour
* Size
* Shape
* Yield
* Quality/duration of storage

Determine which plants are your top-notch candidates by watching them throughout the growing season. Mark them with a coloured stake or ribbon, so that you know they are the ones you want to grab seed from. When you finally collect and prepare the seed for storage, it's helpful to add notes about their characteristics to your label—something like: Hollyhock, pink, rust-resistant.[1]—SN

What does it mean when we talk about seed "vigour"? Why is this important?

You already know about seed viability, which refers to the capability of seeds (including dormant ones that have had their dormancy broken) to germinate under optimal conditions. That means if the seeds are given a suitable temperature, enough oxygen, and water—and, for some, light—they'll sprout.

Seed vigour is a term that describes the quality of seeds in a given sample. The parameters of quality include viability, the percentage of seeds that germinate, the length of time it takes for seeds to germinate, and the strength (hardiness) of the seedlings that are grown. The sample is grown in what are considered "field conditions"—out in your garden bed or in containers on your balcony—wherever your garden is located.

Many factors can influence seed vigour. How the seeds are stored is a big one. (Did you dry them sufficiently, or did they suffer some sort of mechanical damage when you were gathering them that may have harmed the seeds' embryos?) How the seeds develop on the plants they are harvested from is also hugely important. The conditions the plants are grown in before the seeds are gathered and saved make a difference. If the plants experience heavy drought or wild swings in temperature, for example, the seeds they produce may not have a great deal of vigour.

It is essential to note the importance of genetics in determining seed vigour—it's not just about the environment where they developed and the inputs the gardener is able to control.

Keep vigour in mind when you select seed for saving, as it will contribute to the success of future plants.[2]—SN

Why is it important to collect seeds from several different plants of the same variety, not just from a single specimen?

If you save seed from only a plant or two of a single variety in your garden, over successive generations you may initiate a condition called inbreeding depression. This can result in reduced plant vigour, or possibly poor germination (or none at all).

The solution? If you're planning to collect and save seed from a certain type of crop, simply grow several plants of the same variety, not just one or two. That way you'll have more plants to select from. (And, as a bonus, if anyone tells you that you're sowing an awful lot of plants, you can say that you have a responsibility to promote genetic diversity!) Of course, we completely understand that preventing inbreeding depression is more difficult if you have space constraints, but it is worth it to try if you are serious about seed saving and the success of future crops.[3]—SN

When saving seeds, try to collect them from several plants of the same variety instead of just one.

What does it mean to "dry collect" seeds?

Seeds fall into two main categories: wet and dry. Very roughly, wet seeds are those contained in or that are on fruit, and dry seeds are all the rest.

It is fascinating to see all the vastly different forms of dry seeds, from the tiny round ones that are typical of the Brassicaceae, the cabbage or cole family, to the parachutes of dandelions and others in the Asteraceae family, and everything in between. Infinitely interesting is how the seeds are borne on their plants, from the umbels of Apiaceae (the celery, carrot, and parsley family) to the pods of the Fabaceae family (best known for peas, beans, and legumes) and the shakers that spill their mature seed of poppies in the *Papaver* genus.

What is common to all is that the seeds of these species are meant to stay on their plants until fully mature and then disperse via wind, water, animals and birds, or gravity. The plants themselves will be at the end of the season's growth and be ready to die if they are annuals or biennials, to die back to the ground if they are perennials, or, if they are trees or shrubs, to go dormant, with the cycle to resume the following season. When a seed is mature, it is in a dormant state with reduced respiration, which allows dispersal without premature germination.

When collecting dry seed, it is important to plan ahead and select those plants that you are going to keep growing to maturity and to acknowledge that they are going to be looking dry, withered, and ragged by the time their seed is ready. I often will place a "Growing for Seed" tag around the stems of plants I am growing for seed in the community garden as on more than one occasion I have had a helpful person cut such plants back, ending my efforts for the season!

Then the goal is to time your collecting to a T. You want to leave the seed on the plant for as long as possible, but not wait so long that nature has taken a hand and has scattered the seed on the wind, water, or ground, defeating all your efforts.

Some seeds will stay nicely enclosed or attached to a plant and will wait for you to collect them, such as peas and beans in their pods or sunflowers in their seed heads. But experienced collectors will often tie paper bags, muslin bags, or cheesecloth around seed heads as they get close to maturity, especially those that spill their seed readily. This keeps the seeds in the bags if they detach before you can be there. I prefer to cut circles of floating row cover and tie them onto plants, either with string or with a rubber band. I find it works best for me as these circles allow the air in, are lightweight, and dry easily in the event of rain. By the way, these also work to deter squirrels and birds from making off with your sunflower heads.

I also always carry around with me a few sheets of recycled paper and envelopes just in case I find an interesting plant that is ready to share its seed with me. I hold the paper underneath and gently tap the seed heads, and the seed falls neatly onto the paper and then into my envelope.[4]—JM

Calendula is an example of a plant with dry seeds.

Can I collect seed when it is still green on the plant?

Dry seed absolutely must stay on the plant until it is mature. In fact, the best time to collect it is about five minutes before the seed pods open and spill, shoot, or otherwise let fly their seeds.

Green immature seed hasn't yet had the chance to form the dry aril or shell around the embryo inside, or accumulate enough food to sustain that embryo. If the seeds are taken off the plant before maturing, most likely the seeds won't germinate or will have low viability and/or vigour.

Unfortunately, an early cold spell can come on the prairies before your seeds are fully mature. If the seeds have managed to get to their proper size and are already starting to go brown and dry, then you may be able to save those seeds. Make sure to remove entire seed heads from the plant, including some stem, if possible. Lay them out flat on screens or in cardboard boxes in a well-ventilated and warm space and allow them to thoroughly dry. Alternatively, hang them upside down from the rafters. Never dry them in plastic containers as the seed heads will have a lot of moisture content and be very prone to developing diseases. The process can take a few weeks, so do inspect them regularly to make sure there are no signs of mould developing. If seed heads are fleshy, such as those of sunflowers, then turn them regularly so they can dry evenly. Less dense seed heads can be stirred when you inspect them, to ensure even drying.

Once the seed heads are dry you can go to the next step of removing the seeds from the heads, but do check for those that are obviously duds, such as ones that are shrunken, are off-colour, or just plain don't look healthy. Before sowing them next year, take the precaution of doing a germination test beforehand to avoid potential disappointment.[5] —JM

The seeds of this nasturtium are still too green to collect them to save for sowing at a later date, but you can actually eat green nasturtium seeds. Most gardeners prefer to pickle them and treat them as substitutes for capers. They have a peppery taste.

How do you prevent the cross-pollination of insect- or wind-pollinated plants, so that you can save the seed?

Some open-pollinated plants can be isolated, so that they are not cross-pollinated. This way you can save seed that will be true to the parent plant. Mechanical isolation is the best method for home gardeners to use. It's a bit time-consuming but worth it! Fortunately, the method is simple. Put a white organza or tulle bag over the flowers of your plants, tying it on securely. (The bags must be breathable but not have large holes.) Put the bags on your flowers before the buds begin to open. (If the flowers are open, it's too late to bag them.) Once fruit or seed begins to form, you can remove the bags.

If you want to bag a whole plant or a grouping of plants, you need something a little more substantial. If you're comfortable with building your own wooden or wire frame, you can cover it with fabric or fine metal mesh, then plop it over your plants. If you're not handy, plumbing the depths of your local hardware store or garden centre may yield premade frames or cages that you can cover.

Self-pollinating plants won't need help, but you must hand-pollinate the flowers of plants that you have covered. (Examples include leeks, celery, and members of the *Brassica* genus.) Use an artist's paintbrush or a cotton swab to gently collect the pollen from the male plants and transfer it to the female ones. Be sure to cover the plants back up after you are finished!

There are a couple of other methods for isolating your plants to prevent cross-pollination. Distance isolation can be a big problem for home gardeners—we simply don't have the space to provide the distances needed to separate our crops. A bit more achievable is time isolation. Stagger the planting times of two or more different varieties of the same crop, so that they do not flower and set seed at the same time. The key to this is ensuring that there are absolutely no flowers on the crops that are sown earliest when the successive crops are flowering. That way, no cross-pollination can take place.

Finally, you always think you will remember, but trust me, things get busy and you will probably forget, so be sure to label or tag the specific plants you want to save seed from. Remember to grow and collect seed from several plants of the same variety![6] —SN

This 'Flashy Trout Back' lettuce has been bagged in preparation for seed collection.

Is it possible to save seed from biennial vegetables on the prairies? Are there ways to encourage them to overwinter successfully?

It comes as a surprise to a lot of us gardeners that so many of our common vegetables are biennials! We usually eat them that first year and then are amazed when a carrot overlooked at harvest time suddenly appears and starts growing—really growing—and if we leave it be, it makes a huge three-foot (one-metre) plant with umbel flowers that are bee magnets.

Common vegetables that are biennial include beets, cabbage, carrots, cauliflower, celery, chard, kale, kohlrabi, leeks, onions, parsnips, and turnips. Parsley and angelica grown as herbs are biennial, too. Incidentally, there are many biennial ornamental plants hardy to the prairies that we can practise seed saving on. Black-eyed Susan, forget-me-not, foxglove, hollyhock, pansy, primrose, and viola are just a few biennials that you can overwinter and reap a huge harvest without half trying.

The difficulty with saving seed for biennial vegetables lies in getting them to overwinter when they may not necessarily be able to survive being frozen solid. I once tried to overwinter celeriac, thinking that as it is in the carrot family, it might work. All I got was a disgusting mush to dig out the following spring.

There are four general methods you can choose from, depending on how deep the soil in your area typically freezes and what cold storage you have available. The first method is to simply leave the plant in the ground without protection. This is what I did with my celeriac. That said, I have had success this way with other plants, such as carrots, kale, parsley, and parsnips, even when Calgary had a prolonged cold spell in February 2019.

The second method involves leaving the plants in the ground and piling dried leaves or straw overtop in a thick layer. I add a burlap sack or two to anchor the mulch in windy Calgary and pile whatever snow we have overtop for extra insulation. I have overwintered leeks, onions, carrots, and parsnips this way.

The third method involves digging up the plant, including as much of the root

*Swiss chard is an example of a
biennial vegetable. Saving seeds
for biennial plants can be a
challenge on the prairies.*

ball as possible. Snip back the foliage to an inch (2.5 centimetres), but be careful not to touch the crown. Gently brush off soil when it dries, but absolutely make sure that the main root isn't damaged. Allow the roots to cure a bit to toughen the outer skins, then lay them in layers in damp sand in your cold cellar. The temperature needs to be in the range of 40 to 50°F (4 to 10°C). Any warmer, and the roots will have premature sprouting, come March. Most basements are not suitable. Though they can get cold enough in the depths of winter, they warm up as spring comes on. You also need to control humidity as most homes are too dry, which means that the roots will shrivel. However, when humidity is too high, moulds can set in. Oh, for an old-fashioned, earthen cold cellar that is right outside the foundation and that can be accessed through a door in the basement!

Which leads to the last choice. Dig a hole in your garden deeper than the soil usually freezes. In the area below your frost line, place dried leaves in the bottom of the hole, and layer in the plants you want to overwinter. It isn't necessary to bag the plants, but if you do use bags, breathable mesh bags are the best. Pile in more leaves. Then, at the frost line, put in a hard layer as protection for when you unearth them in the spring. Scrap wood or the top of a rubber bin works well. It doesn't do to put your spade through them after all that effort! Pile all the soil back on top, and cross your fingers.

Come spring, wait for the soil to thaw, then lift out the plants, inspect them to make sure they haven't been damaged, and replant them when the air and soil temperatures are suitable, giving them lots of space as they will get much bigger the second year. The same goes for those roots that spent the winter in cold cellars. For those plants under mulch, remove the mulch when it thaws out, and wait to see what happens. Do the same with the "be tough or go home" plants you left out in the elements unprotected, unwittingly or not.

Biennials in the second year, once re-established, will quickly grow foliage, send up flower stalks, and go to seed. By midsummer most will have mature seed, though in my experience, carrots may take all season to mature their seed.

As our median winter temperatures moderate, we are generally having more and more success with overwintering and saving seed from our biennials. It is worth the extra effort involved, and when you are successful, that sense of satisfaction is not to be underestimated![7] —JM

Can you collect the seeds of native plants and seeds from wild spaces?

Collecting native species is entirely possible, and we often do it without realizing it, when we go home after a hike with a few seeds stuck to our socks or pants!

However, there are several rules and guidelines to follow, starting with where you can collect seeds. It is illegal to collect seeds without permission in national, provincial, and municipal parks, and certain natural areas. It is also illegal to collect seeds on private land without permission from the owner. Collecting seeds from public areas, such as transportation corridors or other dangerous areas, is also not wise, as no seed is worth your life.

There are protocols to follow that are encouraged by all nature societies and councils. The most important one is to respect the environment where you are collecting. Many of our natural areas are fragile ecosystems, and we do not want to damage them in pursuit of seed. Wetlands, drylands, and alpine areas are considered the most fragile environments. The exception to this rule is if the area is scheduled for destruction anyway, such as construction sites, where you may get permission to gather seeds before the work begins. Do avoid areas that may be contaminated with weeds, exotic species, or herbicides.

When collecting seeds from a viable ecosystem, take only from areas where there are large stands or populations of a species and then gather only 10 percent of any plant's seeds. If you are collecting seeds over multiple years, make sure to collect from different areas. This will ensure that you amass genetic diversity within your collection.

Many native species are highly specialized and require specific soil and growing conditions to break dormancy and to germinate properly. Keep specific records as to when and where you collected and what the growing conditions were for that season.

Not all native species are suitable for being grown outside their native habitat. Some species may become aggressive and not at all attractive for the home garden. Finally, if you are lucky enough to come across a rare species, do not collect seed from it, but do report its location to your provincial society. They will thank you for the information and work to protect it in situ and hopefully can adopt measures to encourage it to grow and increase its population.[8] —JM

Practice proper seed-collecting etiquette and do not collect the seeds from wild plants such as these found in Kananaskis Country, Alberta.

What precautions must be undertaken when harvesting toxic seeds to save?

Many plants we grow have toxic parts, but their value to us is not diminished—we may love their flowers, for example, or eat the other parts that won't harm us. Rhubarb is one example where one part is edible and another is not: the leaves are toxic, but the leaf stalks (petioles) make the best pie filling you've ever indulged in. Toxicity in plants varies by species. Some can cause minor skin irritation; others, severe burns. Ingestion of certain parts of plants can lead to stomach pain and digestive discomfort, while others can kill you.

Occasionally, the seeds are the toxic parts of the plants, but we still may want to plant them and save them. These seeds may cause serious harm (and possibly death) if ingested, but if they are touched, they can also inflame and severely irritate the skin. A few plants with seeds that shouldn't be handled without protective gear include daphne shrubs (*Daphne* spp.), castor bean (*Ricinus communis*), and gas plant (*Dictamnus albus*). And there are numerous species with leaves and stems that contain chemicals that can cause problems for you when you're working with them to remove seeds. When collecting seeds like these, be sure to cover up all bare skin. Wear long sleeves, pants instead of shorts, and, most importantly, gloves. After you're finished handling the seeds and other toxic plant bits, throw your gloves and clothes into the laundry to remove any oils or residues.

When you purchase seeds or plants, try to learn something about their toxicity, and make a note in your garden journal, so you know to exercise caution when you collect their seeds.—SN

Drying and
Storing Seeds

6

What are some good methods for drying seeds after they have been collected?

Make sure seeds are completely dry before storing them. I like to dry sweet pea pods in small batches in brown paper bags, as the pods burst open when they are completely dry. The bag catches the seeds. Be sure to leave the top of the bag open to promote air circulation—the seeds don't usually fly that far, so they'll stay contained.

Successful seed storage begins and ends with mature, dry seeds—that is, if your seeds are desiccation tolerant (also called orthodox). To make things simple, that's most of what we grow in our prairie gardens, and that's what we will be focusing on here. Desiccation-intolerant (or recalcitrant) seeds, such as those from some aquatic or tropical plants and many trees, do not become dormant when mature and drying can kill them. (Fun fact: there are also semi-recalcitrant seeds, a category that falls between desiccation tolerant and desiccation intolerant.)

A moisture content of more than 10 percent can spell doom for orthodox seeds during storage and ruin all of your hard work in collecting them—not to mention the labour you put into growing the plants that the seeds came from! Dry, properly stored seeds promote better germination rates and increase the length of time a seed is viable. But reaching that magic 10 percent isn't easy if you can't measure it, and most home gardeners do not have the tools to do so.[1]

To ensure your seeds are as dry as you can get them, don't put them in the oven. It's way too tricky to figure out when the seeds are ready in your home kitchen's oven, and you could actually kill them with too much heat. Nix the microwave and the food dehydrator as well, for the same reason.

The best option is to air dry your seeds. Lay them out in a single layer on a flat screen (preferably one in a frame, so you can raise it up a bit off the table, and so that air can flow beneath the screen as well as above it). Flat-bottomed mesh colanders—particularly ones with feet—work well if you don't have a screen. In a pinch, you can use a plate—it just doesn't promote as much air circulation as a screen.

Keep the seeds in a dry location for at least a week, and stir them a few times during that period to expose them to air. If the room you are storing them in is on the humid side, you can try using a fan to move the air around (although don't set the fan to blow directly on the seeds, as you'll have a real mess on your hands).[2] And if you don't get around to packaging them after a week, it's okay to let them sit longer. This process can be as relaxing as you want it to be. After all, you deserve a break after all that weeding you did during the growing season!—SN

Should I use drying agents, such as silica gel and rice, in the containers with my saved seeds?

One aspect of living on the prairies is the fact that our climate is pretty arid—my parched skin in winter can certainly attest to that! Those living in tropical, humid regions have a more difficult time when it comes to sufficiently drying their seeds for storage. Use of reusable, heat-activated silica gel to keep seeds dry is a common practice, and products made from zeolite are under development and are being tested.[3] (I'd recommend saving your rice for cooking.) If you are able to properly dry your seeds on the prairies, you shouldn't need to add any drying agents in your storage containers. However, some gardeners who plan to store their seeds for a longer period of time by placing them in the freezer use silica gel to help get any excess moisture out of the seeds. If you wish to go this route, you can buy packets of silica gel in most craft stores. Look for them in the florist's department, as they're often used to dry flowers. Or, if you happen to like buying shoes (who doesn't?), save all the packages that come in the shoeboxes.

The biggest problem with using silica gel is that it is actually possible to dry your seeds too much, especially if they are small seeds. As home gardeners, we don't have the proper tools to test to see if this has occurred. You can try to avoid this by taking the silica gel out of the seed container after a couple of days, but not using silica gel at all is the best preventive.—SN

What is the best way to clean the chaff and other debris from dry seeds after you've collected them?

When you collect seed, you're inevitably going to end up with other plant parts in the mix—flower heads, perhaps, stems, or leaves. The seeds themselves may be protected by husks or pods. You want to store the seeds, and only the seeds, so you need to sort through all of the plant bits to get at the good stuff.

Only clean seeds from dry plants. Wet plants will not easily clean, and you don't want to be prepping damp seed for storage. A popular method to do the task is to use a screen or a mesh sieve to separate the broken bits of plant debris, called chaff, from the seeds. You can purchase screens specifically designed for this purpose, or build some for yourself. If you really want to do this on the cheap, raid your kitchen for colanders—you might already have something that will work. Use gloved hands to break open pods and rub the plant material across the screen. The mechanical action of breaking open the seed pods or husks is called threshing. Large-scale gardening operations will use a machine to do this—and, of course, it is a process grain farmers know very well. If you have a lot of pods to open, you can try placing them in a cloth bag, tying the bag shut, and smacking it against a hard surface to split open the pods (or you could use a stick to hit the contents of the bag). It takes a bit of practice to know how hard to thresh, because every type of seed is tolerant of a different measure of pressure. (If you thresh the pods too hard, it can cause the seeds inside to shatter.) After you have broken the pods, spread the contents of the bag onto the screen to continue the sorting process.

Manually pick through the chaff, retaining the seeds. If the chaff is smaller than the seeds you are working with, you may be able to push some of the chaff through the screen to discard it. Another option, depending on your set-up, is to push the seeds through the screen instead. Or you can simply pick the seeds out of the debris by hand. Bear in mind that you may need screens with different-sized holes to accommodate various sizes of seeds.[4] Don't chuck the chaff! You can add it to your compost pile or dig it back into the soil.

Another way to separate seeds from chaff is to perform a technique called winnowing. Place plant material on a screen, then manually break open the seed pods

Chaff remains after broccoli seeds have been separated from their pods.

and the seed heads with your gloved hands. If it's a windy day, step outside with the screen, and allow the wind to carry away the light chaff. The seeds should remain on the screen. (Some gardeners use a fan instead of relying on possibly inconstant wind speed.) Winnowing works best with substantial, heavier seeds; lightweight ones may just blow away with the plant debris. —SN

Tomato seeds and other "wet" seeds are usually fermented for storage. How is this done?

Wet seeds are seeds that can be found either inside or attached on the outside of botanical fruit. Plants grow these delectable containers in the hopes that something—be it bird or mammal—will find them irresistible and eat them. Having other species consume the flesh and seeds, digest them, and eliminate them out the other end in a perfect bundle of organic matter for germination is a terrific means of seed dispersal!

Unlike "dry" seeds, these seeds are surrounded by amniotic sacs—a.k.a. "goop"—that are meant to protect the seeds from germinating too early. Once the seeds are eaten, the digestive process erodes the gelid goo surrounding them, making them ready for germination.

When we save wet seeds, we need to remove the sacs unless we plan to use the seeds right away. If not removed, the moisture surrounding the seeds not only will quickly reduce viability, but is a magnet for pathogens to take up residence.

Commercial seed producers remove the sacs with hydrochloric acid, which does the trick but also sterilizes the seeds. Gardeners can process wet seeds by fermenting them. This is a simple process that also provides the seed coats with bacteria, which protects them.

First, choose your fruit, which should be fully mature. You are looking for over-ripe, soft, wizened, or wrinkly fruit, looking like it will just about fall off the plant. Some fruit that will keep ripening off the plant can be harvested earlier, but it will need to fully mature indoors to that stage before you can process the seeds.

Then remove the seeds from the flesh and place them in a container. (You can eat the flesh if you like. I usually cook with it rather than eat it fresh as the flavours are often not optimal.) Fill the container with water and cover it with mesh or cheesecloth so that air can be in contact with the liquid. If fermenting a small batch of seeds, a Mason jar is ideal as the ring serves to anchor the covering, but any container will do, with a rubber band attached to the cover and the top of the container. Set the container to one side in a warm spot where you can see it daily. Some of the flesh and immature seeds will float to the surface. Once you see the liquid bubbling a bit and/or a bit of mould forming on the surface, remove the covering, scoop out the top scum, pour the liquid and the seeds into a fine sieve, and rinse with water until clean. If the seeds have entirely lost their sacs, then you are ready for the next stage. If the seeds still feel slippery, then repeat the entire step.

It is important to dry the freshly fermented seeds quickly. In areas with low humidity, spreading them on a mesh screen does the job, either inside or outside on a warm sunny day, but for those living in a more humid climate, using a dehumidifier can be essential. Do not dry with heat using a dehydrator or an oven as you will only get cooked seeds.

Once you think the seeds are dry, stir them around, and let them dry some more. It is very important to make sure all the moisture is gone before packing the seeds away or they will easily go mouldy.[5] —JM

Ferment wet seeds to remove their amniotic sacs.

Should I store my seeds in the freezer?

You don't have to store orthodox seeds in the freezer, especially if you're planning to sow them in the next year or so. We recommend storing them in a cool, dry environment if you are going to use them within a few years after you collect them. Many gardeners feel that if you want your seeds to stay viable for longer than that, freezing them is the way to go. Generally, seeds that have been stored in a freezer designed for home use could potentially last about five years—and sometimes longer—if you collect the seeds when mature, dry them properly in preparation, and don't open and close the freezer door multiple times a year.[6] (The abrupt fluctuations in temperature will reduce the quality of storage for your seeds.) Drying the seeds so that they have 10 percent moisture content or less is critical. Excess water in the seeds will cause ice to form, and you definitely don't want that to happen. Bear in mind that for home gardeners, it is nearly impossible to measure the amount of moisture in your seeds; most of us do not have the testing equipment.

And what about the refrigerator? Many gardeners do this, and you can certainly experiment: if you can keep the seeds in the back of the fridge, where the temperature is coldest and least affected by the constant trips to grab milk and juice, you may be successful.[7]

Finally, what if you forget to bring your seeds indoors from the garden shed and they overwinter out there? If they're orthodox, mature, and dried properly, they may be okay for sowing the next spring, but wild temperature swings and the potential for moisture can tip the balance—and not in your favour. Store-bought seeds may fare a bit better than those you've collected yourself, because they have been properly dried. It is recommended to do a viability test to check (see pages 23–25), as you might be able to salvage something. I've talked to gardeners who keep their seeds out in the shed all year long and end up successfully germinating some of them, but it's not an ideal situation. Seeds are valuable, and your gardening efforts will be better rewarded if you store them properly.—SN

What types of packages should I store seeds in?

Paper or glassine envelopes get our vote, hands down. Airtight plastic, glass, or metal containers are excellent choices as well. Your airtight container can be anything from an empty pill bottle or a Mason jar to a small plastic tote. Re-purpose or recycle where you can, but make sure your containers are all squeaky clean and perfectly dry.

Alternatively, consider a combo for the ultimate in organization: if you grow ten different types of beans, and you collect seeds from all of them, put them in envelopes, and then place the envelopes in an airtight container marked "Beans." Another good organizational idea: slip your seed envelopes into a photo album, designating one sleeve for each envelope. I've seen other gardeners use paper file boxes to great effect, filing the seed envelopes under alphabetized headers, as you would important documents.

Ensure everything is labelled with the name of the plant (including the cultivar) and the date the seeds were collected. (If you want, add in details such as the location of the plants, what colour the flowers were, how large the yield was that year, or any other information you think you may want to know later on. Of course, you can also keep a separate gardening journal for just such a purpose.) Grouping the seed packages by plant type and/or alphabetizing them is handy for retrieval as well. When you're eager and ready to sow, you don't want to be wondering where all your seeds are! —SN

*Repurposed airtight glass
containers are suitable for
storing seeds.*

*We couldn't have
said it better
ourselves!*

What is a seed exchange, and why are they valuable?

A seed exchange is the sharing of extra seeds between one gardener and another over a fence or a cup of coffee. But it is really much more than that simple act.

Gardeners are a passionate and generous bunch. We love to share ideas and knowledge as well as physical things like seeds or tools. Exchanging our seeds builds a community through acts of generosity and the curiosity to find out how those seeds worked out for the recipient. Sharing our seeds helps to conserve the varieties we collect. As they are grown by others, new seeds from each season are collected and then shared on. Sharing our seeds helps build diversity of seed varieties since they are grown in different circumstances. Ultimately, seed exchanging is also about ensuring that seeds—literally the necessities for our survival—remain in the public domain, available to every person, and are not held by specific entities.

Many seed exchanges are organized affairs by garden clubs, community gardens, and other organizations. There are also online seed exchanges, where members of an exchange can send seeds to each other for no more than the cost of postage. Another wonderful way to participate in a seed exchange is by attending a Seedy Saturday event (which can take place on any day of the week or month, but most often they occur on Saturdays in the spring).

In general, seeds that are exchanged are open-pollinated varieties rather than hybrid varieties. All seeds should be labelled with the plant name (both common and botanical), year grown, the gardener's name, and where the seed was grown. Sometimes growing notes or information about whether viability tests have been conducted on the seeds is included. You don't need fancy packaging for seeds you share as long as there is somewhere to include the necessary information. If you haven't had the opportunity to take part in a seed exchange, be sure to do so at your earliest opportunity. They are a ton of fun!—JM & SN

Acknowledgements

Janet and Sheryl would like to extend a massive thank you to the publishing team at TouchWood Editions: Taryn Boyd (publisher), Kate Kennedy (editorial coordinator), Paula Marchese (copy editor), Tori Elliott (marketing and publicity coordinator), Tree Abraham (designer), Meg Yamamoto (proofreader), and Pat Touchie (owner). We are so grateful to all of you for helping us realize this dream!

From Janet:

What a grand journey to be on with Sheryl beside me. I literally wouldn't be on this journey without her. Long may we tread this road together!

My profound gratitude and love for all the people behind me providing love, support, and the odd boost when I need it the most. It means so much to me. Especially my family who have cooked the dinners, cleaned up around me, and even watered the garden throughout the process.

To all those gardeners, brand new and old wise ones, with your questions to challenge me and advise, tips and tricks to absorb—my grateful thanks! I love learning along with you and from you. Not a day goes by that I don't learn something in and about gardening, mostly from you all!

From Sheryl:

I'm so delighted you've taken on this project with me, Janet! It's an absolute honour to work with you!

I am sending out love and hugs to all of my family and friends for their support and encouragement. I can't thank you enough!

I also want to thank all the prairie gardeners I've had the pleasure of chatting with over the years—whether online, in community gardens, or through volunteer work. Your dedication, passion, and enthusiasm for growing plants is absolutely inspiring.

Notes

Introduction

1. Delevoryas, "Gymnosperm," Encyclopaedia Britannica.

2. Jacquot, "Seeds, from the Largest to the Oldest to the Safest," *Discover*.

Chapter One

1. Heistinger, *The Manual of Seed Saving*, 21.

2. Richerson, *The Complete Idiot's Guide to Seed Saving and Starting*, 6–12; Jeffery, *Seedswap*, 18–19; Hole, "A Lesson in GMO, Hybrid and Heirloom Garden Seeds," *Edmonton Journal*; Bassett, "The Breed of Your Seed: Understanding the Difference between Open-Pollinated, Hybrid, Heirloom and GMO," Northeast Organic Farming Association Massachusetts Chapter (website); Iannotti, "Difference between Heirloom, Hybrid, and GMO Vegetables," The Spruce (website); Warmflash, "'Hybridization Is Not Genetic Modification'—And Other Scientifically Suspect Anti-GMO Sayings," Genetic Literacy Project (website); Mattern, "Hybrid Seeds vs. GMOs," *Mother Earth News*.

3. Pegplant (website), "GMO or GE Seeds? What's the Difference?"

4. Pegplant (website), "GMO or GE Seeds? What's the Difference?"

5. Richerson, *The Complete Idiot's Guide to Seed Saving and Starting*, 11–12; Jeffery, *Seedswap*, 20–21; Hole, "A Lesson in GMO, Hybrid and Heirloom Garden Seeds," *Edmonton Journal*; Bassett, "The Breed of Your Seed: Understanding the Difference between Open-Pollinated, Hybrid, Heirloom and GMO," Northeast Organic Farming Association Massachusetts Chapter (website); Government of Canada, "About Novel and Genetically-Modified (GM) Foods"; Government of Canada, "Completed Safety Assessments of Novel Foods Including Genetically Modified (GM) Foods"; University of Saskatchewan College of Agriculture and Bioresources, "Heirloom Seeds and GMO Seeds: Don't Get Caught Up in the Marketing Hype."

6. Just Food (website), "Seed Saving Projects"; *Seeds of Diversity*, "The 100-Year-Old Tomato—Alacrity."

7. Wild About Flowers (website), "Non-native Annual Wildflower Mixes versus Native Perennial Wildflower Mixes"; Wild About Flowers (website), "What to Expect When Seeding Native Perennial Wildflower Mixes"; Alberta Native Plant Council (website and PDF), "Guidelines for the Purchase and Use of Wildflower Seed Mixes"; Hines, "Wildflower Seed Mixes Include Some Wicked Bloomers," University of Washington; Crain, "You've Got Your Bee Wildflower Seed Mix, What Now?," The Nature Conservancy at Cornell University; Invasive Species Council of Manitoba (website), "Terrestrial Species."

8. Capon, *Botany for Gardeners*, 27–33; The Learning Garden (website), "From Seed to Seed: Stages of Germination."

9. Henderson, "Seed Saving Time: The Float Test," Show Me Oz (website).

10. Clear Creek Seeds (website), "Seed Viability Chart"; Johnny's Select Seeds (website), "Seed Storage Guide."

11. West Coast Seeds (website), "Pelleted Seeds"; Growing for Market (website) and Johnny's Seeds, "Pelleted Seeds for Accurate Sowing, Reduced Thinning"; Betz, "Pelleted versus Raw Seed," High Mowing Organic Seeds (website).

12. Pavlis, "Why Do Beets Always Need to Be Thinned?," Garden Fundamentals (blog).

13. University of Kentucky College of Agriculture, Food and Environment, "Seed Ecology"; C. Shock, Cheatham, Harden, Mahony, and B. Shock, "Sustainable Wildflower Seed Production: Germination; Seed Dormancy," Oregon State University College of Agricultural Sciences, Malheur Agricultural Experiment Station.

14. Richerson, *The Complete Idiot's Guide to Seed Saving and Starting*, 110–11; Hatter, "How to Scarify Seeds," Garden Guides (website); American Meadows (website), "How to Scarify Seeds for Spring Planting."

15. American Meadows (website), "How to Cold Stratify Seeds for Spring Planting."

16. Richerson, *The Complete Idiot's Guide to Seed Saving and Starting*, 106.

17. Ellis, *Starting Seeds*, 59.

18. Richerson, *The Complete Idiot's Guide to Seed Saving and Starting*, 126–27; Vanderlinden, "How to Determine the Proper Depth to Plant Seeds," The Spruce (website); You Should Grow (website), "5 Fatal Mistakes for Growing Seeds."

19. Iannotti, "Seeds That Need Light for Good Germination," The Spruce (website); Science and Plants for Schools, "Why Do Some Seeds Germinate Only in the Dark?"

20. University of Saskatchewan College of Agriculture and Bioresources, "Growing Your Own Transplants."

21. Quish, "Seeds Sprouting Inside a Tomato," University of Connecticut College of Agriculture, Health and Natural Resources Extension; Newton, "Why Are Tomato Seeds Sprouting Inside of My Tomato?," North Carolina Cooperative Extension; Baessler, "What Is Vivipary—Reasons for Seeds Germinating Prematurely," Gardening Know How (website); Lerner, "In the Grow: Question and Answer," Purdue Extension.

Chapter Two

1. *The Old Farmer's Almanac*, "Planting Calendar for Edmonton, AB"; Sproule, "Your Seeding Calendar," Salisbury Greenhouse (website); Garden Retreat (website), "Seed Starting Dates for Calgary."

2. Richerson, *The Complete Idiot's Guide to Seed Saving and Starting*, 120–21; Kelley, Sellmer, and Lamont, "Homemade Potting Media," Penn State Extension; Schoellhorn, "The Dirt on Dirt—Potting Soil," Proven Winners (website).

3. Coleman, "Ditch the Pots, Use Soil Blocks!," Chelsea Green Publishing (website).

4. *Garden Culture*, "Should You Sterilize Potting Soil?"; Harrington, "Do Potting Soils Need to Be Sterilized Before Use?," SFGate (website); Pavlis, "Sterile Soil—Does It Really Exist?," Garden Myths (blog).

5. Pavlis, "Seedling Heat Mats—Are They Needed?," Garden Myths (blog).

6. Halleck, *Gardening Under Lights*, 21–26, 45–78.

7. Ellis, *Starting Seeds*, 51.

8. Richerson, *The Complete Idiot's Guide to Seed Saving and Starting*, 125.

Chapter Three

1. Bartok, "Horizontal Air Flow Is Best for Greenhouse Air Circulation," University of Massachusetts at Amherst, Center for Agriculture, Food and the Environment.

2. Richerson, *The Complete Idiot's Guide to Seed Saving and Starting*, 146–47; Turner, *Seed Sowing and Saving*, 21–22; BBC Gardening Guides (website), "About Pricking Out."

3. Turner, *Seed Sowing and Saving*, 13; Iannotti, "Damping Off Disease of Seedlings," The Spruce (website); Encyclopaedia Britannica, "Damping-off."

4. GrowOrganic.com (website), "Soil Temperature Basics: What's the Best for Transplanting Vegetable Starts and Seedlings?"

Chapter Four

1. Seeds Now (website), "How Do I Know Which Seeds to Direct Sow and Which Seeds to Start Indoors?"

2. Iannotti, "What 'Days to Maturity' Means for Your Plants," The Spruce (website); Hodges, "Understanding the Seed Packet," University of Nebraska Lincoln Extension, Institute of Agriculture and Natural Resources; Hodgins, "Spring Planting: It's Important to Understand the 'Days to Maturity' Number on Seed Packages," *London Free Press*.

3. Erker and Brick, "Legume Seed Inoculants," Colorado State University Extension; Rhoades, "Organic Gardening Soil Inoculants—Benefits of Using a Legume Inoculant," Gardening Know How (website); Van d'Rhys, "To Inoculate or Not to Inoculate?," Dave's Garden (website).

4. Manitoba Agriculture Office, "Agricultural Climate of Manitoba"; Government of Alberta, "Frost-Free Period 1971–2000"; *The Old Farmer's Almanac*, "First and Last Frost Dates."

5. The Old Farmer's Almanac, "How to Keep Birds Away from Your Garden"; Anderson, "12 Effective Ways to Keep Birds Out of the Vegetable Garden," Lovely Greens (website).

6. *The Old Farmer's Almanac*, "Planting Calendar for Edmonton, AB"; Sproule, "Your Seeding Calendar," Salisbury Greenhouse (website); Garden Retreat (website), "Seed Starting Dates for Calgary."

7. Dupont, "Seed and Seedling Biology," Penn State Extension; Albert, "Vegetable Seed Germination Temperatures," Harvest to Table (website); Jauron, "Annual Flower Seed Germination Guide," Iowa State University Extension and Outreach, Horticulture and Home Pest News.

8. Mitchell, "10 Vegetables to Plant Now for a Bountiful Spring Harvest," Inhabit (website); Nardozzi, "Planting in the Fall for a Spring Bounty," *Mother Earth Living*; Rhoades, "How to Pre-seed Your Garden in Fall for an Early Spring Harvest," Gardening Know How (website).

Chapter Five

1. Charbonneau, "Seed Saving: Selecting Plant Characteristics," Southern Exposure Seed Exchange (website).

2. Oregon State University Seed Laboratory, "Importance of Seed Vigor Testing."

3. Thompson-Adolf, *Starting & Saving Seeds*, 44.

4. Gough and Moore-Gough, *The Complete Guide to Saving Seeds*, 40–43; Heistinger, *The Manual of Seed Saving*, 46.

5. Roth, "Collecting and Storing Seeds," *Fine Gardening*; Salt Spring Seeds (website), "How to Save Seeds."

6. Thompson-Adolf, *Starting & Saving Seeds*, 47–49.

7. Salt Spring Seeds (website), "How to Save Seeds"; Wildfong, "Saving Seeds of Biennial Vegetables," *The Canadian Organic Grower*; Gardenerdy (website), "List of Biennial Plants."

8. Native Plant Society of Saskatchewan (website), "Recommendations for the Collection and Use of Native Plants"; Hammermeister, "Native Seed Harvesting and Marketing," Native Plant Society of Saskatchewan (website and PDF); Alberta Native Plant Council (website and PDF), "Plant Collection Guidelines for Horticultural Use of Native Plants."

Chapter Six

1. Pavlis, "Should Collected Seed Be Stored in the Fridge or Freezer?," Garden Myths (blog).

2. Wildfong, "How to Dry Your Seeds to Perfection," Seeds of Diversity (website).

3. University of California at Davis Feed the Future Innovation Lab for Horticulture, "Drying Beads Save High Quality Seeds."

4. BC Farms and Food (website), "Six Ways to Screen and Winnow Seeds: Low-Tech Tools for Threshing Seeds."

5. Heistinger, *The Manual of Seed Saving*, 43–45; Richerson, *The Complete Idiot's Guide to Seed Saving and Starting*, 38–40; Ashworth, *Seed to Seed*, 26; Ashwanden, "Seed Saving, Part 2: Practical Ways to Save Seed," Permaculture Research Institute (website); Bonsall, "The Seed Series: Techniques for Saving Dry vs. Wet Seeds," Chelsea Green Publishing (website).

6. Scott, "Home Seed Saving and Storage," Terroir Seeds (website).

7. Pavlis, "Should Collected Seed Be Stored in the Fridge or Freezer?," Garden Myths (blog).

Sources

Albert, Steve. "Vegetable Seed Germination Temperatures." Harvest to Table (website). harvesttotable.com/vegetable-seed-germination-temperatures/.

Alberta Native Plant Council (website and PDF). "Guidelines for the Purchase and Use of Wildflower Seed Mixes." June 2006. anpc.ab.ca/wp-content/uploads/2015/01 /wildflower_seeds_guidelines.pdf.

———. "Plant Collection Guidelines for Horticultural Use of Native Plants." April 3, 2007. anpc.ab.ca/wp-content/uploads/2015/01/gardener_guidelines.pdf.

American Meadows (website). "How to Cold Stratify Seeds for Spring Planting." Accessed July 20, 2020. americanmeadows.com/blog/2018/03/07/how-to-cold-stratify -seeds.

———. "How to Scarify Seeds for Spring Planting." Accessed April 8, 2020. americanmeadows.com/blog/2017/06/05/how-to-scarify-and-soak-seeds-for-spring -planting.

Anderson, Tanya. "12 Effective Ways to Keep Birds Out of the Vegetable Garden." Lovely Greens (website). June 5, 2018. lovelygreens.com/ways-to-keep-birds-out-of-the -garden/.

Ashwanden, Charlotte. "Seed Saving, Part 2: Practical Ways to Save Seed." Permaculture Research Institute (website). November 14, 2014. permaculturenews .org/2014/11/14/seed-saving-part-2-practical-ways-to-save-seed/.

Ashworth, Suzanne. *Seed to Seed: Seed Saving and Vegetable Techniques for Vegetable Gardeners.* 2nd ed. Decorah, IA: Seed Savers Exchange, 2002.

Baessler, Liz. "What Is Vivipary—Reasons for Seeds Germinating Prematurely." Gardening Know How (website). Last updated April 9, 2018. gardeningknowhow.com /garden-how-to/propagation/seeds/what-is-vivipary.htm.

Bartok, John W., Jr. "Horizontal Air Flow Is Best for Greenhouse Air Circulation." University of Massachusetts at Amherst, Center for Agriculture, Food and the Environment. May 2005. ag.umass.edu/greenhouse-floriculture/fact-sheets/horizontal -air-flow-is-best-for-greenhouse-air-circulation.

Bassett, Christy. "The Breed of Your Seed: Understanding the Difference between Open-Pollinated, Hybrid, Heirloom and GMO." Northeast Organic Farming Association Massachusetts Chapter (website). February 2019. nofamass.org/articles/2019/02/breed -your-seed-understanding-difference-between-open-pollinated-hybrid-heirloom.

BBC Gardening Guides (website). "About Pricking Out." Accessed April 10, 2020. bbc.co.uk/gardening/basics/techniques/propagation_pricking1.shtml.

BC Farms and Food (website). "Six Ways to Screen and Winnow Seeds: Low-Tech Tools for Threshing Seeds." September 5, 2015. bcfarmsandfood.com/six-ways-to -screen-and-winnow-seeds/.

Betz, Paul. "Pelleted versus Raw Seed." High Mowing Organic Seeds (website). Accessed February 25, 2020. highmowingseeds.com/blog/pelleted-versus-raw-seed/.

Bonsall, Will. "The Seed Series: Techniques for Saving Dry vs. Wet Seeds." Chelsea Green Publishing (website). Accessed February 25, 2020. chelseagreen.com/2015/seed-saving-dry-and-wet/.

Capon, Brian. *Botany for Gardeners*. 3rd ed. Portland, OR: Timber Press, 2010.

Charbonneau, Jordan. "Seed Saving: Selecting Plant Characteristics." Southern Exposure Seed Exchange (website). February 26, 2019. southernexposure.com/blog/2019/02/seed-saving-selecting-plant-characteristics/.

Clear Creek Seeds (website). "Seed Viability Chart." Accessed April 8, 2020. clearcreekseeds.com/seed-viability-chart/.

Coleman, Eliot. "Ditch the Pots, Use Soil Blocks!" Chelsea Green Publishing (website). Accessed April 9, 2020. chelseagreen.com/2020/ditch-the-pots-use-soil-blocks/.

Crain, Rhiannon. "You've Got Your Bee Wildflower Seed Mix, What Now?" The Nature Conservancy at Cornell University. March 21, 2017. content.yardmap.org/learn/beyond-wildflower-mixes/.

Delevoryas, T. "Gymnosperm." Encyclopaedia Britannica. Accessed April 5, 2020. britannica.com/plant/gymnosperm.

DuPont, S. Tianna. "Seed and Seedling Biology." Penn State Extension. Last updated August 28, 2012. https://extension.psu.edu/seed-and-seedling-biology.

Ellis, Barbara. *Starting Seeds: How to Grow Healthy, Productive Vegetables, Herbs and Flowers from Seed*. North Adams, MA: Storey Publishing, 2013.

Encyclopaedia Britannica. "Damping-off." Accessed April 10, 2020. britannica.com/science/damping-off.

Erker, B., and M.A. Brick. "Legume Seed Inoculants." Colorado State University Extension. September 2014. extension.colostate.edu/topic-areas/agriculture/legume-seed-inoculants-0-305/.

Garden Culture. "Should You Sterilize Potting Soil?" December 11, 2015. gardenculturemagazine.com/sterilize-potting-soil/.

Gardenerdy (website). "List of Biennial Plants." Accessed April 13, 2020. gardenerdy.com/list-of-biennial-plants.

Garden Retreat (website). "Seed Starting Dates for Calgary." June 24, 2013. buyagreenhouse.com/gardening-information/seed-starting-dates-for-calgary.

Gough, Robert, and Cheryl Moore-Gough. *The Complete Guide to Saving Seeds: 322 Vegetables, Herbs, Fruits, Flowers, Trees, and Shrubs*. North Adams, MA: Storey Publishing, 2011.

Government of Alberta. "Frost-Free Period 1971–2000." Last updated March 10, 2020. open.alberta.ca/dataset/760b719d-1904-4750-8ac6-db2e65ef6ab2.

Government of Canada. "About Novel and Genetically-Modified (GM) Foods." Last modified February 25, 2020. canada.ca/en/health-canada/services/food-nutrition/genetically-modified-foods-other-novel-foods.html.

————. "Completed Safety Assessments of Novel Foods Including Genetically Modified (GM) Foods." Last updated May 7, 2020. canada.ca/en/health-canada /services/food-nutrition/genetically-modified-foods-other-novel-foods/approved-products .html#wb-auto-5.

Growing for Market (website) and Johnny's Selected Seeds. "Pelleted Seeds for Accurate Sowing, Reduced Thinning." January 2012. growingformarket.com/articles /Pelleted-Seeds-for-Accurate-Sowing-Reduced-Thinning.

GrowOrganic.com (website). "Soil Temperature Basics: What's the Best for Transplanting Vegetable Starts and Seedlings?" April 11, 2012. groworganic.com/blogs /articles/soil-temperature-for-transplanting-vegetable-starts-and-seedlings.

Halleck, Leslie F. Gardening Under Lights: The Complete Guide for Indoor Growers. Portland, OR: Timber Press, 2018.

Hammermeister, Andy. "Native Seed Harvesting and Marketing." Native Plant Society of Saskatchewan (website and PDF). September 2000. npss.sk.ca/docs/2_pdf/NPSS _NativeSeedHarvestingandMarketing.pdf.

Harrington, Jenny. "Do Potting Soils Need to Be Sterilized Before Use?" SFGate (website). Accessed April 9, 2020. homeguides.sfgate.com/potting-soils-need-sterilized -before-use-71003.html.

Hatter, Kathryn. "How to Scarify Seeds." Garden Guides (website). September 21, 2017. gardenguides.com/86284-scarify-seeds.html.

Heistinger, Andrea. The Manual of Seed Saving: Harvesting, Storing, and Sowing Techniques for Vegetables, Herbs, and Fruits. Portland, OR: Timber Press, 2013.

Henderson, Jill. "Seed Saving Time: The Float Test." Show Me Oz (website). August 12, 2016. showmeoz.wordpress.com/2016/08/12/seed-saving-time-ripe-seeds-and-the -float-test/.

Hines, Sandra. "Wildflower Seed Mixes Include Some Wicked Bloomers." University of Washington. April 18, 2002. washington.edu/news/2002/04/18/wildflower-seed-mixes -include-some-wicked-bloomers/.

Hodges, Laurie. "Understanding the Seed Packet." University of Nebraska Lincoln Extension, Institute of Agriculture and Natural Resources (PDF). September 2009. extension.unl.edu/statewide/fillmore/Seeds.pdf.

Hodgins, Denise. "Spring Planting: It's Important to Understand the 'Days to Maturity' Number on Seed Packages." London Free Press. Last modified January 28, 2015. lfpress.com/2015/01/28/spring-planting-its-important-to-understand-the-days-to -maturity-number-on-seed-packages/wcm/fdf4cee3-34be-41f2-dfcd-8181123732b1/.

Hole, Jim. "A Lesson in GMO, Hybrid and Heirloom Garden Seeds." Edmonton Journal. March 13, 2015. edmontonjournal.com/lesson+hybrid+heirloom+garden+seeds /10887301/story.html.

Iannotti, Marie. "Damping Off Disease of Seedlings." The Spruce (website). Last updated June 10, 2020. thespruce.com/damping-off-disease-of-seedlings-1402519.

————. "Difference between Heirloom, Hybrid, and GMO Vegetables." The Spruce (website). Last updated July 25, 2019. thespruce.com/hybrid-vs-heirloom -vegetables-1403361.

————. "Seeds That Need Light for Good Germination." The Spruce (website). Last updated March 19, 2020. thespruce.com/seeds-that-need-light-for-good -germination-1403091.

————. "What 'Days to Maturity' Means for Your Plants." The Spruce (website). Last updated October 2, 2019. thespruce.com/what-does-days-to-maturity-mean-1402471.

Invasive Species Council of Manitoba (website). "Terrestrial Species." Accessed April 5, 2020. invasivespeciesmanitoba.com/site/index.php?page=terrestrial-species.

Jacquot, Jeremy. "Seeds, from the Largest to the Oldest to the Safest." Discover. March 7, 2009. discovermagazine.com/environment/seeds-from-the-largest-to-the-oldest-to-the -safest.

Jauron, Richard. "Annual Flower Seed Germination Guide." Iowa State University Extension and Outreach, Horticulture and Home Pest News. February 25, 2000. hortnews.extension.iastate.edu/2000/2-25-2000/annflowgerm.html.

Jeffery, Josie. Seedswap: The Gardener's Guide to Saving and Swapping Seeds. Boston: Roost Books, 2014.

Johnny's Select Seeds (website). "Seed Storage Guide." Last updated December 20, 2017. johnnyseeds.com/on/demandware.static/-/Library-Sites-JSSSharedLibrary/default /dw913ac4d0/assets/information/seed-storage-guide.pdf.

Just Food (website). "Seed Saving Projects." Accessed April 5, 2020. justfood.ca/seed -saving-projects-and-events/.

Kelley, Kathleen M., James C. Sellmer, and Phyllis Lamont. "Homemade Potting Media." Penn State Extension. Last updated October 22, 2007. extension.psu.edu /homemade-potting-media.

The Learning Garden (website). "From Seed to Seed: Stages of Germination." Last updated 2001. garden.org/onlinecourse/Part15.htm.

Lerner, B. Rosie. "In the Grow: Question and Answer." Purdue Extension. March 4, 2010. agriculture.purdue.edu/agcomm/newscolumns/archives/ITG/2010 /March/100305ITG.html.

Manitoba Agriculture Office. "Agricultural Climate of Manitoba." Accessed April 11, 2020. gov.mb.ca/agriculture/weather/agricultural-climate-of-mb.html.

Mattern, Vicki. "Hybrid Seeds vs. GMOs." Mother Earth News. January 16, 2013. motherearthnews.com/real-food/hybrid-seeds-vs-gmos-zb0z1301zsor.

Mitchell, Beverley. "10 Vegetables to Plant Now for a Bountiful Spring Harvest." Inhabit (website). November 15, 2016. inhabitat.com/10-vegetables-to-plant-now-for-a -bountiful-spring-harvest/.

Nardozzi, Charlie. "Planting in the Fall for a Spring Bounty." Mother Earth Living. September/October 2016. motherearthliving.com/gardening/vegetable-gardening /planting-in-the-fall-zmgz16sozolc.

Native Plant Society of Saskatchewan (website). "Recommendations for the Collection and Use of Native Plants." Accessed April 13, 2020. npss.sk.ca/docs/2_pdf /Recommendations_for_the_Collection_and_Use_of_Native_Plants.pdf.

Newton, Shannon. "Why Are Tomato Seeds Sprouting Inside of My Tomato?" North Carolina Cooperative Extension. Last updated July 11, 2018. hoke.ces.ncsu .edu/2018/07/why-are-tomato-seeds-sprouting-inside-of-my-tomato/.

The Old Farmer's Almanac. "First and Last Frost Dates." Accessed April 11, 2020. almanac.com/gardening/frostdates.

————. "How to Keep Birds Away from Your Garden." April 14, 2017. almanac.com /content/how-keep-birds-away-your-garden.

————. "Planting Calendar for Edmonton, AB." Accessed April 11, 2020. almanac .com/gardening/planting-calendar/AB/Edmonton.

Oregon State University Seed Laboratory. "Importance of Seed Vigor Testing." Accessed April 11, 2020. seedlab.oregonstate.edu/importance-seed-vigor-testing.

Pavlis, Robert. "Seedling Heat Mats—Are They Needed?" Garden Myths (blog). Accessed April 9, 2020. gardenmyths.com/seedling-heat-mats/.

————. "Should Collected Seed Be Stored in the Fridge or Freezer?" Garden Myths (blog). Accessed January 12, 2020. gardenmyths.com/storing-collected-seed-fridge-or -freezer/.

————. "Sterile Soil—Does It Really Exist?" Garden Myths (blog). Accessed April 9, 2020. gardenmyths.com/sterile-soil-really-exist/.

————. "Why Do Beets Always Need to Be Thinned?" Garden Fundamentals (blog). Accessed April 8, 2020. gardenfundamentals.com/why-beets-need-thinning/.

Pegplant (website). "GMO or GE Seeds? What's the Difference?" January 21, 2015. pegplant.com/2015/01/21/gmo-or-ge-seeds-whats-the-difference/.

Quish, Carol. "Seeds Sprouting Inside a Tomato." University of Connecticut College of Agriculture, Health and Natural Resources Extension. June 4, 2014. blog.extension .uconn.edu/2014/06/04/seeds-sprouting-inside-a-tomato/#.

Rhoades, Heather. "How to Pre-seed Your Garden in Fall for an Early Spring Harvest." Gardening Know How (website). Last updated May 8, 2018. gardeningknowhow .com/edible/vegetables/vgen/preseeding-vegetables.htm.

————. "Organic Gardening Soil Inoculants—Benefits of Using a Legume Inoculant." Gardening Know How (website). Last updated April 5, 2018. gardeningknowhow.com/edible/vegetables/beans/soil-inoculants.htm.

Richerson, Sheri Ann. The Complete Idiot's Guide to Seed Saving and Starting. New York: Alpha Books, 2012.

Roth, Sally. "Collecting and Storing Seeds." Fine Gardening, issue 60. Accessed February 25, 2020. finegardening.com/article/collecting-and-storing-seeds.

Salt Spring Seeds (website). "How to Save Seeds." Accessed February 25, 2020. saltspringseeds.com/pages/how-to-save-seeds.

Schoellhorn, Rick. "The Dirt on Dirt—Potting Soil." Proven Winners (website). Accessed April 9, 2020. provenwinners.com/learn/dirt-dirt-potting-soil.

Science and Plants for Schools. "Why Do Some Seeds Germinate Only in the Dark?" Accessed April 8, 2020. saps.org.uk/saps-associates/browse-q-and-a/659-why-do-some -seeds-germinate-only-in-the-dark.

Scott, Stephen. "Home Seed Saving and Storage." Terroir Seeds (website). Accessed January 12, 2020. underwoodgardens.com/seed-saving-and-storage/.

Seeds Now (website). "How Do I Know Which Seeds to Direct Sow and Which Seeds to Start Indoors?" Accessed April 10, 2020. seedsnow.com/blogs/news/143255111-how -do-i-know-which-seeds-to-direct-sow-and-which-to-seeds-to-start-indoors.

Seeds of Diversity. "The 100-Year-Old Tomato—Alacrity." March 2016. seeds.ca /d/?t=33df029400002951.

Shock, C.C., N.E. Cheatham, J.L. Harden, A.C. Mahony, and B.M. Shock. "Sustainable Wildflower Seed Production: Germination; Seed Dormancy. Oregon State University College of Agricultural Sciences, Malheur Agricultural Experiment Station. Accessed April 8, 2020. agsci.oregonstate.edu/mes/sustainable-wildflower-seed -production/germination-seed-dormancy.

Sproule, Rob. "Your Seeding Calendar." Salisbury Greenhouse (website). Accessed April 11, 2020. salisburygreenhouse.com/your-seeding-calendar/.

Thompson-Adolf, Julie. Starting & Saving Seeds: Grow the Perfect Vegetables, Fruits, Herbs, and Flowers for Your Garden. Minneapolis: Cool Springs Press, 2018.

Turner, Carole B. Seed Sowing and Saving: Step-by-Step Techniques for Collecting and Growing More Than 100 Vegetables, Flowers, and Herbs. Pownal, VT: Storey Publishing, 1998.

University of California at Davis Feed the Future Innovation Lab for Horticulture. "Drying Beads Save High Quality Seeds." Accessed January 12, 2020. horticulture .ucdavis.edu/information/drying-beads-save-high-quality-seeds.

University of Kentucky College of Agriculture, Food and Environment. "Seed Ecology." Accessed April 8, 2020. uky.edu/hort/sites/www.uky.edu.hort/files/pages -attachments/Dormant%20seeds.pdf.

University of Saskatchewan College of Agriculture and Bioresources. "Growing Your Own Transplants." February 2, 2018. gardening.usask.ca/articles-how-to/growing-your -own-transplants.php.

———. "Heirloom Seeds and GMO Seeds: Don't Get Caught Up in the Marketing Hype." February 26, 2018. gardening.usask.ca/articles-how-to/heirloom-seeds-and-gmo -seeds.php.

Vanderlinden, Colleen. "How to Determine the Proper Depth to Plant Seeds." The Spruce (website). Last updated October 18, 2019. thespruce.com/how-deeply-should -seeds-be-planted-2539711.

Van d'Rhys, Darius. "To Inoculate or Not to Inoculate?" Dave's Garden (website). Last updated April 1, 2015. davesgarden.com/guides/articles/printstory .php?rid=2429&bn=%2Farticles%2Fview%2F2429.

Warmflash, David. "'Hybridization Is Not Genetic Modification'—And Other Scientifically Suspect Anti-GMO Sayings." Genetic Literacy Project (website). November 17, 2015. geneticliteracyproject.org/2015/11/17/hybridization-is-not-genetic -modification-and-other-scientifically-suspect-anti-gmo-sayings/.

West Coast Seeds (website). "Pelleted Seeds." Accessed February 25, 2020. westcoastseeds.com/blogs/glossary/pelleted-seeds.

Wild About Flowers (website). "Non-native Annual Wildflower Mixes versus Native Perennial Wildflower Mixes." Accessed April 5, 2020. wildaboutflowers.ca/points_to _ponder_detail.php?Non-Native-Annual-Wildflower-Mixes-versus-Native-Perennial -Wildflower-Mixes-12.

———. "What to Expect When Seeding Native Perennial Wildflower Mixes." Accessed April 5, 2020. wildaboutflowers.ca/points_to_ponder_detail.php?What-to -expect-when-seeding-Native-Perennial-Wildflower-Mixes-9.

Wildfong, Bob. "How to Dry Your Seeds to Perfection." Seeds of Diversity (website). September 2016. seeds.ca/d/?t=09c1012100003118.

———. "Saving Seeds of Biennial Vegetables." The Canadian Organic Grower. January 2004. magazine.cog.ca/article/saving-seeds-biennial-vegetables/.

You Should Grow (website). "5 Fatal Mistakes for Growing Seeds." Accessed April 8, 2020. youshouldgrow.com/mistakes-germinating-seeds/.

Index

Page numbers in italics refer to photographs.

About the Authors

SHERYL NORMANDEAU was born and raised in the Peace Country region of northern Alberta and has made Calgary her home since 1994. A writer and master gardener, Sheryl holds a bachelor's degree in English, as well as a Prairie Horticulture Certificate and an Urban Sustainable Agriculture Certificate. Since 2013, she has served as the online Ask an Expert for the Calgary Horticultural Society. She works at the Calgary Public Library—besides gardening, books of all kinds are her grand passion! She is a small-space gardener (on a tiny balcony and in a plot in a nearby community garden) and she is most enthusiastic about growing veggies. She lives with her husband, Rob, and their rescue cat, Smudge. Find Sheryl at Flowery Prose (floweryprose .com) and on Facebook (@FloweryProse), Twitter (@Flowery_Prose), and Instagram (flowery_prose).

JANET MELROSE was born in Trinidad, West Indies, and immigrated to Canada in 1964. She has lived in Calgary since 1969. She is a master gardener and the creator and owner of the successful horticulture business Calgary's Cottage Gardener, which specializes in garden education, horticultural therapy, and advocating for sustainable local food systems. She holds bachelor's degrees in sociology and history, a Prairie Horticulture Certificate, and a Horticultural Therapy Certificate. Janet is a lifelong gardener, coming from a heritage of English gardening. She has a large garden at home in the suburbs of Calgary that can only be described as a typical cottage garden. She cares for eight other gardens throughout Calgary through her work as a horticultural therapist, as well as a bed at the Inglewood Community Garden. She is married to Steve (for a long time), and they have two children, Jennifer and David. Three cats, Patrick, Theo, and Mia, currently own their home and patrol against the deer, hares, squirrels, skunk, mice, and assorted birds that believe the garden is theirs, too! Connect with Janet on Facebook (@calgaryscottagegardener), Twitter (@CalCottageGrdnr), and Instagram (CalgarysCottageGardener).

About the Series

It looks like you've discovered the **Guides for the Prairie Gardener.** This budding series puts the combined knowledge of two lifelong prairie gardeners at your grubby fingertips. Whether you've just cleared a few square feet for your first bed of veggies or are a seasoned green thumb stumped by that one cultivar you can't seem to master, we think you'll find Janet and Sheryl the ideal teachers. Find answers on seeds, soil, trees, flowers, weather, climate, pests, pots, and quite a few more. These slim but mighty volumes, handsomely designed, make great companions at the height of summer in the garden trenches and during cold winter days planning the next season. With regional expertise, elegance, and a sense of humour, Janet and Sheryl take your questions and turn them into prairie gardening inspiration. For more information, and for other titles in the series, visit touchwoodeditions.com/guidesprairiegardener.

The Prairie Gardener's Go-To for
Vegetables

JANET MELROSE　　SHERYL NORMANDEAU

The Prairie Gardener's Go-To for
Pests & Diseases

JANET MELROSE　　SHERYL NORMANDEAU

The Prairie Gardener's Go-To for
Seeds

JANET MELROSE　　SHERYL NORMANDEAU

The Prairie Gardener's Go-To for
Small Spaces

JANET MELROSE　　SHERYL NORMANDEAU